JOHN PO
AND
LORETTA BRADY, M.S.W.

P9-CRC-076

Will
The
Real Me
Please
Stand
Up?

25 Guidelines for Good Communication

TABOR
PUBLISHING

Allen, Texas

Acknowledgments

The Twelve Steps reprinted with permission of Alcoholics Anonymous World Services, Inc.

Copyright 1949 by E. E. Cummings. Reprinted from "now all the fingers of this tree(darling)have" in his volume *Complete Poems 1913-1962* by permission of Harcourt Brace Jovanovich, Inc., and GRAFTON BOOKS A Division of the Collins Publishing Group.

"Charade" written by Henry Mancini and Johnny Mercer. © 1963 Northridge Music Co. and Northern Music Ltd. All rights reserved. Used by permission.

Photo Credits

All photos except page iv: Jean-Claude Lejeune
Page iv: Chris Smith

Cover design: Tricia Legault

Calligraphy: Bob Niles

Copyright © 1985 by John Powell, S.J.

All rights reserved. No part of this book shall be reproduced or transmitted in any form or by any means, electronic or mechanical, including photocopying, recording, or by any information or retrieval system, without written permission from the Publisher.

Send all inquiries to:
Tabor Publishing
One DLM Park
Allen, Texas 75002

Library of Congress Catalog Card Number: 85-72665

Printed in the United States of America

ISBN 1-55924-283-3

1 2 3 4 5   94 93 92 91 90

About the Authors
and Pronouns . . .

The ideas and expressions in this book have a history of evolution. Loretta Brady is a psychotherapist in private practice, and John Powell teaches at Loyola University in Chicago.

They have incorporated into this book their separate thoughts and their experiences in counseling and the classroom.

They have also collaborated in the presentation of this material in workshops given over the past several years.

For the sake of a smoother flow in reading, no distinction is made in these pages between when Loretta is speaking and when John is speaking. There are a few exceptions and these are clearly identified.

What is Real?

"What is REAL?" asked the Rabbit one day, when they were lying side by side near the nursery fender, before Nana came to tidy the room. "Does it mean having things that buzz inside you and a stick-out handle?"

"Real isn't how you are made," said the Skin Horse. "It's a thing that happens to you. When a child loves you for a long, long time, not just to play with, but REALLY loves you, then you become Real." . . .

"It doesn't happen all at once," said the Skin Horse. "You become. It takes a long time. That's why it doesn't often happen to people who break easily, or have sharp edges, or who have to be carefully kept. Generally, by the time you are Real, most of your hair has been loved off, and your eyes drop out and you get loose in the joints and very shabby. But these things don't matter at all, because once you are Real you can't be ugly, except to people who don't understand."

from *The Velveteen Rabbit* by Margery Williams

Contents

PART FOUR: General Practices That Promote Good Interpersonal Communication

INTRODUCTION

Communication between any two human beings is admittedly difficult. When we communicate, we share something. As a result this something becomes a common possession. For example, if I communicate a joke or recipe, this act of sharing will make the joke or recipe our common possession; we will possess something together. But this sharing of an item or a thing is not the communication or sharing about which we hope to write. Through human, relational communication what we gain as a common possession is: *ourselves.* Through our acts of sharing or communication we know and we are known. You share the gift of yourself with me, and I share the gift of myself with you. It is this human, relational communication that we will be speaking about in these pages.

It seems obvious that human communication is the lifeblood and heartbeat of every relationship. It also seems clear that the gift of self through the sharing of self-disclosure is *the essential gift* of love. All other gifts—the jewelry, colognes, flowers, and neckties—are only tokens or symbols. The real gift of love is the gift of self.

Somehow we sense that our lives seem to go about as well as our relationships. We are about as happy as our relationships are happy. A "human loner" is a contradiction in terms. The existence of a human in isolation from others is like a plant trying to survive without sunlight or water. No new growth can occur, and the life that does exist begins to wither and will slowly die. For us to be is to be with another or with others. The quality of our human existence is grounded in our relationships.

But for all this, human communication does not have a good track record. Many people, even many married couples, seem to be involved in relating to one another without the kind of deep mutual knowledge that is the result of good communication. Many of us settle for a truce, an accommodation rather than a real relationship.

At the end of the movie *Kramer vs. Kramer,* I felt an impulse to stand up in the theater and protest. I wanted to tell the Kramers: "You don't really need a divorce. What you really need is to get to know each other. You need to learn how to communicate. You are both good and decent people, but you don't seem to realize and appreciate the goodness and giftedness of each other." It is said that " Art imitates life," and unfortunately there are very many real life situations like the one portrayed in *Kramer.* Many of us worry about relationships coming to an end. "Breaking up is hard to do," according to the song lyrics. Maybe a greater concern should

*The quality of our human existence
is grounded in our relationships.*

be that our relationships never have a real beginning or enjoy true growth. Maybe we are too ready to settle for a charade, while we wonder about what could be.

To further complicate the achievement of real relationships, there is the problem of fantasy or imagination. Picture, if you will, two people trying to communicate with each other. If the communication were represented graphically, it might well look like a wire or wires stretching between the two persons. The traffic of communication moves both ways, so the sharing that passes through the connecting wires moves from person A to person B and from B to A. But all around the material actually transmitted is an embroidery of fantasy or imagination. We fantasize far beyond the actual communication. Imagination always takes over where actual communication ends.

For example, I say to you, "You know, I don't think that you look your best when you wear your hair that way." Let us presume that this is all I said and this is all I meant. But you almost can't help imagining other things that you suspect are implied in my remark. "I don't think he likes me; it's not just my hairstyle." Or you could imagine, "He is just getting back at me because I told him that the color of his suit was not flattering." These are only possible examples of the dangers of fantasy. What is certain is that where communication leaves off, fantasy or imagination takes over. Very often this works to our own great harm.

Another example. Somehow I am sure that everyone with whom you or I have had prolonged contact has a rather definite idea about whether we like them or not. Very likely we have never explicitly told them how we actually feel. But somehow imagination filled in for the facts, and imagination almost always distorts the facts. When a man is helping a woman on with her coat, his hand may accidentally brush against her cheek. She may imagine that this was deliberate and enter into a whole unreal (literally fantastic) relationship. "He touched me! And after that nothing seemed the same. I'm sure he intended it. It is a clear signal: he loves me." The poor man in question would be very surprised to learn all this. He thought he was just helping her on with her coat. (Until she tells him, "I know you love me!")

Or a woman sitting at the same table with a man may accidentally move her foot against his under the table. He may easily imagine that it was deliberate. He interprets it as a secret but certain sign, saying what words can never say. "She is playing 'footsie' with me! I think she is in love with me." Such imaginings can lead us into a sad world of delusion. The crash at the end is always painful.

It seems obvious that the more frequently we use exact verbal communication, the less room there is for imagined messages and consequent misunderstanding. It is when we keep our true thoughts and feelings veiled—when we play games, wear masks, and pretend certain postures—that others are left to imagine our meanings. Misunderstanding always results, usually with disastrous consequences.

Clear verbal communication not only spares us this unnecessary suffering of misunderstanding. More positively, it results in deep and lasting relationships. And relationships are the source of our growth as persons. Paul Tournier, the Swiss physician and author, has wisely suggested what many of us believe. For a person to achieve his or her full potential there must be at least one other person with whom he or she is totally open and feels totally safe at the same time. We are social beings. We are in this together. For us to be all that we can be, deep and permanent relationships are necessary. And to accomplish such relationships effective communication is absolutely essential.

It has been said that a work of art is first and foremost a *work*. Relationships work for those who work at them. Unquestionably, the main work of a real relationship is communication. Communication slowly brings about deep and clearly defined relationships, but only if we keep working at it. Like any other human accomplishment, communication is a matter of continued practice. All the verbal formulas are useless unless practice has made the skills of communication a part of us. There is no formula for success that works unless we do.

Most of us learned to talk in the first year or two of life. And, according to the neonatologists, we began to hear even before birth. Unfortunately, most of us think that because we learn to talk and to hear, we automatically learn to communicate. That is like saying that because I can touch the keys of a piano, I will automatically play melodious music. Good communication is not an automatic or easy achievement. Think about your own problems in understanding and in being understood. It is a fact that good communication is never really achieved until two people decide to work at it. We must learn by study and practice the difficult art of communication. We must learn to recognize and avoid the pitfalls. (And if you agree, we think that this book or one like it is for you!)

What we would like to do in the following pages is provide a simplified statement and explanation of the attitudes and skills that seem to promote effective human sharing. With some of these attitudes and skills there may be an immediate recognition and acceptance. Others may prove more challenging. But all will need repeated practice until they become a matter of habit.

That's how we learned to play the piano or ride a bicycle. It was the same for us with the rules of grammar. We had to practice these rules until they became habitual. However, once repeated practice had made the rules "a part of us," we could talk freely and confidently. Somehow I am sure that if we practice the ground rules of good communication described in this book, they will become a matter of instinct and habit. Then we will be able to communicate ourselves more accurately and to relate to others much more freely and confidently. And this is essential if we are to experience the happiness of a full life.

We have often heard the complaint that psychology has been preoccupied with sick people, always investigating the sources of mental and emotional sickness. But recently there has been a new trend to study healthy and happy people, and to investigate the sources of human happiness and health. My own experience, observation, and research has led me to believe that communication is the most important of all the sources of happiness and health. Communication is the essential foundation of our happiness.

When people begin to communicate effectively, a total change begins which ultimately affects all the areas of life. The senses seem to come alive. Color that was never noticed before is newly appreciated. Music that was not heard before becomes an accompaniment of life. Peace that was never before experienced begins to find its place in the human heart. Of course, the only proof is experiential. To know the truth of all this, you have to try it. As the old saying goes, "Try it. You might like it."

The suffering of noncommunication in a relationship is a very real and painful suffering. Often in our human relationships the lines of communication are poorly erected, and they fall quickly during the crisis of a storm. The result is loneliness, the scourge of the human spirit. But when these lines are established again, it is like a second springtime of love and joy and all good things. Health and happiness of spirit begin to blossom in this springtime of communication.

Recently a woman in southern Illinois approached me with the exciting statement that I had saved her life. Since I had never seen this woman before, I naturally had to ask a few questions. She explained that several years and several children after her marriage, she had a mental breakdown and was hospitalized. After rest and medication she was discharged into the care of a psychiatrist. Being a very simple woman, she readily admitted that she did not understand what the doctor was trying to tell her. So she remained close to the edge of another breakdown. Then she added, "One day the doctor gave me your book, *Why Am I Afraid to Tell You Who I Am?* I read it and realized that I could have my feelings, that I could and must share my feelings with others."

She continued, "Well, anyway, I started to do this. At first my poor husband did not know what had happened. I had come to life. I wasn't a statue anymore. But more important, I started to feel better. Soon I didn't need my doctor or medicines anymore. That was several years ago, and right now I am happily raising my children and I'm a volunteer helper at the local hospital. For the first time in my life I really feel alive."

More recently a man told me his life story. He shared the trauma of his parents' divorce when he was seven. When his constant prayer for their reconciliation was apparently unanswered, he decided to "be a devil." Although there were evidences of a deep goodness that was never lost, he insisted that his life had been consumed in going astray and taking others with him. Eventually he married, but after fathering three children, he got sick of marriage and family and "wanted out." "I told my wife I wanted a divorce, that I had had it. I resented any questions about my reasons. All I knew was that my guts were aching.

"Then somebody suggested a communication weekend, sponsored by the Marriage Encounter movement. In the writing and sharing of that weekend, thirty years of repressed pain and resentment poured out of me. In the last sharing, I wrote constantly for an hour and a half. I wrote a small volume. Once the floodgates came down just a little, there was no stopping me. In the wake of the weekend, I felt as though thirty years of painful personal history had been lifted from my shoulders. I felt free and whole again. It was really the first day of the rest of a new life for me."

These two stories are true, but they are only two of many such experiences. The effects of communication are so obvious and immediate that I have now come to think of communication as the beginning of all real change. It is the essential nourishment of human health and the only doorway to a new and happy life.

There is still another very valuable benefit of learning and practicing the skills of good communication: *personal maturity*. If we truly believe the truths and accept the attitudes that underlie honest and open communication, we will come into a healthy contact with reality. Having given up our roles and games, we will soon be dealing more effectively with ourselves as we really are and others as they really are. We will begin to be authentic and true to ourselves and to others. The obvious result of all this is maturity.

No one (including myself) likes to be immature, but in fact we all are. We are beings in process, and we have not yet arrived at all that we can be. The absolute condition of our human growth is this contact with reality. And honest, open communication is the only street that leads us into the real world. The only alternative is to accept a life that is only an act, a meaningless pretense.

The chapters to follow describe the assumptions, attitudes, and practices that make for effective human communication. But this book needs more than a simple reading. Like the rules of grammar or the techniques of typing, the guidelines of good communication require practice. Only when they have become instinctual and habitual will we begin to enjoy deep and permanent relationships. We will then begin to grow as never before. And once we are on this road, happiness cannot be far away.

The question of communication may be the most important question you or I have ever considered.

PART ONE

Assumptions and Attitudes Necessary for Good Communication

1

We must be committed to communication.

The beginning of all successful communication is desire — the desire to communicate. This desire cannot be vague and negotiable. It has to be a flint-hard posture of the will, an inner resolution, a firm promise made to ourselves and to others with whom we are trying to relate.

I am determined to work at this, to give it all I've got. This commitment is unconditional: no fine print in the contract, no "ifs" or "buts" or time limits. I will work at it when it is easy and when it is difficult. I will try to tell you who I am. And I will listen to learn who you are. I will do this when I feel like it and even when I don't feel like it. I promise to hang in there with you even when the child in me would rather play games, pout, or punish you. I promise to hang in there even when I feel like quitting. Together we will work at sharing until we have built strong lines of communication. Only then can we experience the personal fulfillment that comes with effective communication.

All this may sound as though the commitment to communication requires a *will* of blue steel. The truth of the matter is that there is no such thing as a strong will. What is strong or weak in us is *motivation.* When someone is highly motivated, such a person will seem to have a strong and determined will. But the secret of willpower is the power of motivation. Tell a person that he or she must give up smoking or die, and suddenly the will seems to be infused with great strength. Actually it isn't the will that has grown strong. The will reacts in direct proportion to the motives proposed and perceived.

If a person really wants to live, the threat of death can be a powerful motivation. We humans can do unbelievable things if we are sufficiently motivated. Almost always a motive takes the form of escape from pain or anticipation of reward. When the presence of pain makes our lives seriously uncomfortable, we are motivated to change. Or when the rewards for accomplishment seem sufficiently great, we are motivated to pay the price and earn those rewards.

And so it is supremely important for you and me to ask: Do I really want to communicate? What are the pains and penalties if I don't? What are the rewards if I do? These may well be among the most important questions we will ever ask ourselves.

The difficulty of proposing motivation is that different motives appeal to different people. Some people are greatly attracted to the "limelight," while others just want to be left alone in anonymity. Some of us are highly motivated by personal appearance. We get enough rest and do not overeat because we want to "look good." Others of us couldn't care less about personal appearance.

However, there are some things that all of us find very painful, like loneliness. Loneliness is the prison of the human spirit. When we are lonely, we pace back and forth in small, shut-in worlds. We believe that no one understands us and we don't really care very much about understanding others. On the other side of the coin, most of us have at least fleetingly experienced the joy of sharing. Maybe we have stood with another on the shore of an ocean, watching a gorgeous sunset. It meant so much to be able to turn to another and say, "Isn't it beautiful!" Or we may have shared a secret joy or pain with another. We remember the profound consolation of feeling understood. It felt so good to know that someone cared, that we were not alone.

In other words, there is a reward system and a sanction system built into human nature. We have an inner need to know and to be known, and the satisfaction of this need brings us a sense of human fulfillment. When we build walls of separation between ourselves and others, our immediate inner reaction might be a sense of security. But the eventual result is starvation of spirit, a pervasive sense of loneliness. We have built our own prisons. We care about no one and no one cares about us. We are alone.

Nevertheless, human experience is highly personal. Each of us experiences intimacy and loneliness in a unique and highly personal way. And so each one of us must somehow describe his or her personal motivation to communicate. It would be very helpful at this time to make a listing of our motives: the needs, desires, drives, pains, and pleasures. Remember our will is only as strong as our motivation. The probability of success is only as great as our grasp of the forces that are moving us toward our desired goals.

However, before you make a list of the motive forces that move you to communication, it might be helpful to recall other things to which you have been committed. Do you remember resolving to lose weight, to give up smoking, to

learn how to play a musical instrument, to get a college degree or a certain job? Recall the driving forces (the motivation) that braced and strengthened your resolution. Maybe this is too obvious to mention, but the best *reasons* to do something may not be the most forceful *motives* for you or me. For example, the best reasons for giving up smoking or losing weight might be health related. But some of us might be more forcibly motivated by the fact that smoking leaves an odor in our clothes or obesity looks bad in a bathing suit.

So, with that windup, here's the pitch: Make a list of the things that impel you to communication. Remember that the best reasons are not always the best motives. Remember, too, that your motives are the backbone of your commitment. Unless we are really committed, there will be little real communication. There will be a painful loneliness. However, if we are truly committed, we will eventually succeed, and find the fullness of life.

Paul Tournier maintains that it is this inner desire, this determination, that lies at the center of all successful communication. In his book *To Understand Each Other,* he tells the story of two people who wanted to communicate but had no language in common. By gestures, pictures, sign language, and other creative means they managed to accomplish a successful exchange. They eventually understood each other, but only because they really wanted to communicate.

Commitment is clearly a matter of priorities. We all know the importance of priorities from personal experience. If we

Loneliness is the prison of the human spirit.

have five things to get done in one day, we somehow manage to accomplish only those things to which we have given priority. We do those things to which we attach a special sense of importance. So it is important and wise to list, to reflect upon, and to rehearse our personal motives. If we want good communication badly enough, we will give it high priority. And if we give it high priority, we will achieve success.

Once a commitment has been made, the main obstacle to perseverance is *failure.* It is a common human experience that failure obscures and weakens a commitment. We decide to go on a diet. Our determination pulses strongly. Our willpower is fueled by clear motives and emotional enthusiasm. Then we fail. We eat a high-caloric dessert. And suddenly we find ourselves on an eating binge. The throbbing sense of commitment, the pulsation of motives, the emotional enthusiasm all seem like a distant and vague dream that was dreamed a long time ago.

It is important to remember that the way to success for us humans is usually paved with failures. Abraham Lincoln lost at least several elections before he was finally elected president. Thomas Edison experimented for two years on many materials from all over the world before he discovered a usable filament for the electric light bulb. When Marconi suggested the possibility of wireless transmission of sound (the radio), he was committed to a mental institution. But people like Lincoln, Edison, and Marconi were strongly motivated. So they didn't give up. They somehow knew that the only real failure is the one from which we learn nothing. They seemed to go on the assumption that there is no failure greater than the failure of not trying, and so they continued to try in the face of repeated failures.

There is a definite "failure syndrome" that can become the cancer of communication. We set out to share, to know, and to be known. Of course, we tend to romanticize to some extent the process that produces intimacy between two searching human beings. Then there is a misunderstanding. Suddenly the collaborators in the magnificent work of communication become contestants in the arena of a win-lose struggle. In win-lose contests everyone loses. And sadly, once the tug-of-war begins, there is an immediate sense of emotional frustration. Unchecked, this frustration quickly turns into anger and aggression. Then there is projection of blame, even if it isn't verbalized. "It's your fault. You started it." There is no longer a comforting sense of sharing, but only a seething sense of hostility.

The discouragement of such setbacks seems to turn many of us away from our commitment to communication. We rationalize that communication with this partner is impossible or that profound sharing happens only in romantic novels, not in real life.

Lou Holtz, the football coach at the University of Notre Dame, has publicly insisted that the key to success in any enterprise is commitment. He admits that in the first years of his marriage he was looking for "a way out." Then he discovered that the problem wasn't with his marriage, but within himself. He was not deeply committed to making it work. And marriage works only for those who work at it. Later, he tried his hand at coaching professional football (the New York Jets). "Let's go see what it is like," he said to his family. He did see what it was like, and hindsight revealed to this honest man that he did not really want it, that he was not really committed to it. So he eventually returned to college coaching. Holtz insists that he has learned this truth: All human success is the result of a persistent commitment.

So it seems that the first thing we must explore in ourselves is our personal understanding of and desire for good communication. We must ask ourselves honestly about our priorities. Is communication important to me? If I were to list the ten top priorities of my life at this time, would communication make my list? Do I really want to know and to be known? Are there bogus fears that communication will end tragically? If I were to share myself honestly with another, what do I fear might happen? Someone has humorously said that nine out of every ten human problems result from poor communication. The tenth results from good communication. If I had to describe my "catastrophic fear" of good communication, the worst thing that could possibly happen, what would it be? What do I see as the greatest danger in total openness and honesty?

A good friend of mine was a Navy Air Corps pilot during the Second World War. He tells me that studies reveal that the most successful pilots could be recognized before they ever got into a plane. It seems that prospective pilots were asked to fill out a questionnaire. The one most important question (and answer) that infallibly predicted success (or failure) was this: "How badly do you want to be a Navy Air Corps pilot?" Clearly, desire and determination are the roots of all human success.

So we leave you to ponder the question at hand: How badly do you want to communicate? If you really want it, and are willing to work at it, success is not far away from you. And the rewards of success are personal growth, effective and good relationships, and in the end the happy life which all of us are seeking.

The only way to know how much you want something is to try it. After you begin to do something, the depth of your desire will be clear.

2

*We must be convinced that we are a gift to be
given, and that through their self-disclosure
others are a gift offered to us.*

Somerset Maugham wrote in *The Razor's Edge:*

> For men and women are not only themselves; they are
> the region in which they were born, the city apartment
> in which they learned to walk, the games they played
> as children, the old wives' tales they overheard, the
> food they ate, the schools they attended, the sports
> they followed, the poems they read, and the God they
> believed in.

Sometimes we don't feel like it, but each of us is a unique
mystery. The mystery of you and the mystery that is me have
never existed before. No one exactly like you or me will ever
exist again. The combination of qualities and giftedness that
is you is a package that has never been put together before.
It is as unique as your fingerprints. And only you can share
your mystery and giftedness with me. It is also true that just
as every snowflake and every grain of sand on the seashore
has a unique structure, so am I different from every other
human being in all of human history. The treasure of my
uniqueness is mine to give or to withhold.

The poet e. e. cummings once wrote:

> and now you are and i am now and we're
> a mystery which will never happen again.

If you choose to withhold your gift from me, I will be
deprived of sharing in the unique mystery and experience of

you. Likewise, I can deny you the vicarious experience of what it is like to be me. Just as we will forever be deprived by such mutual withholding, the opposite possibility is also true. We can be forever enriched by a mutual openness and sharing. The vicarious participation in another's unique human existence is always enriching. This is the great gift of communication.

When you tell me who you are, when you share with me your uniqueness, you will take me into a different world, a different time and place, a different family. You will share your old neighborhood with me, and tell me the stories that you listened to as a child. You will take me into valleys and to the tops of mountains I have never seen. You will lead me into the secret vaults of experiences that were not part of my life. You will introduce me to emotions, hopes, and dreams that were never mine. And this can only widen the dimensions of my mind and heart. I will be forever enriched by our sharing. The size of my experienced world will be permanently enlarged because of your goodness to me.

Most people don't feel this way. It is a very common anticipation that "if I open up to you, I will burden you."

My self-disclosure
will make no other demands on you
but to take my sharing
into the gentle and grateful hands of acceptance.
In giving you this gift
I am truly giving you myself.
It is my most precious,
perhaps my only true gift.

Some have said the same thing from a different perspective: "People don't want to hear about me. They have enough problems of their own." Can this be true?

Self-disclosure in and of itself is never a burden. It is important to realize that in and of myself I am a gift. If I give you this gift as an act of love through honest self-disclosure, it will not be a burden. It will be the unconditional gift of *communication.* Gifts are never burdens, unless strings are attached. My sharing will ask nothing of you except an empathic listening. My self-disclosure will make no other demands on you but to take my sharing into the gentle and grateful hands of acceptance. In giving you this gift I am truly giving you myself. It is my most precious, perhaps my only true gift.

Some time ago I was given an anonymous piece, called "Persons Are Gifts." I would like to paraphrase parts of it here.

Persons are the gifts of God to me. They are already wrapped, some beautifully and others less attractively. Some have been mishandled in the mail; others come "Special Delivery." Some are loosely wrapped; others very tightly enclosed.

But the wrapping is not the gift, and this is an important realization. It is so easy to make a mistake in this regard, to judge the contents by the cover.

Sometimes the gift is opened very easily; sometimes the help of others is needed. Maybe it is because they are afraid. Maybe they have been hurt before and don't want to be hurt again. It could be that they were once opened and then discarded. They may now feel more like "things" than "human persons."

I am a person: like everyone else I too am a gift. God filled me with a goodness that is only mine. And yet

*sometimes I am afraid to look inside my wrapping.
Maybe I am afraid I would be disappointed. Maybe I
don't trust my own contents. Or it may be that I have
never really accepted the gift that I am.*

*Every meeting and sharing of persons is an exchange
of gifts. My gift is me; your gift is you. We are gifts to
each other.*

Some months ago a sad-looking man approached me at a
convention. He told me that he had read many of my books,
but admitted to having one lingering doubt. "Why should I
tell you who I am? What good would it do?" I appealed to the
supposed Irish privilege of answering a question by asking
one. "Do you think I would be enriched if you were to share
your story with me?" "Oh," he shook his head sadly, "I can't
imagine that." "Aha!" I responded in my own awkward
attempt at shock therapy, "that's where you're wrong."

Sometimes I fear that most of us are like that dear old man.
We think we have to have a star-studded, Fourth of July story
to tell. We imagine that a real gift should bear the scent of
roses and have gold embroidery at its edges. The truth is that
any human story, if shared with another as an act of love, will
widen the mind and warm the heart of that person.

I can recall several instances in which people whom I just
didn't like (but tried to love) opened up to me and left me
gasping for air. One dear old man, with a crusty exterior and
a flinty manner, confided to me that everything he had ever
attempted had ended in failure. He gave me chapter and verse
of one devastating failure after another. He ended by
admitting, "I've sure been a damned fool, haven't I? I took to
attacking others so they would be distracted from my own
history of failure. I guess I figured that the best defense was a
good offense."

I learned very much from him about the human heart and the meaning of a broken human spirit. I know that I have become more tolerant, less anxious to judge or label others because this good man once shared his "dubious" gift with me.

Persons really are gifts, aren't they?

3

We must be determined to be honest with ourselves.

The late Dag Hammarskjold, once the secretary-general of the United Nations, suggested that we have become adept at exploring outer space, but that we have not developed similar skills in exploring our own personal inner spaces. In fact, he wrote: "The longest journey of any person is the journey inward." And in *Hamlet,* Act 1, Scene 3, the aged Polonius gives this advice to his son, Laertes:

This above all: to thine own self be true;
And it must follow, as the night the day,
Thou canst not then be false to any man.

At first the advice to be honest with myself seems superfluous. I want to ask, How can I lie to myself? And yet the gurus of communication insist that the first obstacle to communication with another is not an obstacle between myself and that other person. The first obstacle is encountered within myself. It is obvious that if I am not telling myself the truth, I certainly cannot tell you the truth. I can't tell you what I am not telling even myself. If I am not in touch with the feelings and attitudes that are within me, it will be impossible for me to share them with you. If I am deceiving myself, I will certainly deceive you.

Rather early in his career as a psychiatrist, Sigmund Freud discovered that each of us actually has three levels of the mind: (1) the *conscious* (which includes the perceptions of which we are aware from moment to moment); (2) the *preconscious* or *subconscious* (which is the storage center for materials that can be recalled when needed); and (3) the *unconscious* (the storehouse for those memories, impulses, and emotions we cannot comfortably live with). Freud thought that the conscious and preconscious levels were relatively unimportant because the unconscious exerts so much more influence in our lives. A friend of mine who is a psychiatrist once speculated that 90 percent of our motivation is drawn from the unconscious level of the mind.

As noted, the conscious mind rather obviously contains only our present perceptions. The subconscious level of the mind is the storage center for materials that we can bring up into the conscious mind when needed. For example, most of us can recall the multiplication tables if and when needed. But the unconscious is the storehouse for those memories, emotions, and motives that we "just can't live with." It has been called the basement of the mind where "eyesores" are stored. These are buried deep within us. Unfortunately, they are buried alive, not dead. And so they continue to influence us. The burial process is called repression. Repression is not a conscious or deliberate process. We bury our unwanted belongings without even realizing it or remembering them.

I do not like you, Dr. Fell,
The reason why I cannot tell.
But this I know, and know full well,
I do not like you, Dr. Fell.

Repression into our unconscious minds always tends to throw us off balance. We develop unconscious prejudices and biases. An inferiority complex is one such prejudice. It is possible that this self-directed prejudice began in early childhood with parental neglect, but the conscious mind is not aware of this. However, our way of viewing things, our choice of words, our "Freudian slips" of the tongue, and even our accidents may all be the result of things we are repressing.

Another example. An older child may spend a lifetime resenting a younger brother or sister because "you took my mommy away from me. I was getting all the attention and affection before you came along." Such resentment could linger in the unconscious for a lifetime, providing motivation for vindictive meanness and an anger that will squirt out at strange times and for seemingly strange reasons. In this case the older child will never consciously realize the source of his or her aversion as long as it remains buried in the unconscious. To the extent that we repress we lose contact with ourselves.

Fortunately, the realities that we have repressed into the unconscious are always trying to surface for recognition. They are something like wood held under water. However, if we welcome self-knowledge, they will gradually surface. The important thing is to want to know what is in us. We must cultivate the desire to be honest with ourselves.

Honesty with oneself is a habit of self-awareness that must be practiced daily. And this self-awareness is more a process than a simple fact. We must habitually try to become aware of the highly personal and individual way that we function in processing our sensations, perceptions, emotions, and motives. We must look more carefully at the way we come to our decisions and ultimately to our actions. The general process is this:

1. First of all, our senses daily take in a million bits of data (the things we see, hear, touch, taste, and smell). Part of self-awareness is to become more consciously aware of these sensations.

2. Then we organize these sensations into mental perceptions or ideas. We should try to understand better our personal way of doing this.

3. From our perceptions result our emotions. Our thinking usually controls the way we feel. Consequently, these emotions or feelings, our joys and sorrows, can tell us much about our thinking and ourselves, if we are willing to learn. Obviously, feelings in themselves are neither good nor bad, but they are symptomatic. They tell us a lot about how we organize and interpret our sense data into perceptions.

4. Then there is the question of our motives. It is a psychological truism that we do everything for a reason, but often that reason is hidden from us. Searching for and recognizing these motives is an essential part of self-awareness.

5. By what process do we come to our inner decisions? Each of us does this differently. Some of us are more controlled by our feelings; others by intellectual perceptions and motives. Some are more influenced by programming; others by personal experiences of the past.

6. And finally, how do we choose to express these inner decisions in action? For example, I may inwardly decide to continue harboring a grudge against you. Then I choose to express this inner decision by refusing to talk to you. Why did I choose to act out my grudge by pouting?

In order to be honest with ourselves we must continually seek a deeper awareness of the individual way we proceed through these six steps. Only in this way will we gain an increased awareness of our personal processes, and a more conscious control over our actions and reactions. We must, of course, all through this process take responsibility for our own decisions and behavior. We know that they are the result of something in us. At the same time we must be listening and looking to find out what that something is. We must be trying to learn who we really are rather than trying to tell ourselves who we should be.

A good beginning might be to develop an increased awareness of my chosen "act" or "role." Why do I choose to wear this "mask" of mine? Why each of us chooses the act, the role, the mask we do may always remain something of a mystery. However, we should try to locate the roots of this choice. And even though this act or role may have several variations and differ during various periods of life, there is always a "payoff" of some kind. My act or role helps me cope with reality, and attain whatever it is that I am seeking. My act

We must be trying to learn who we really are rather than trying to tell ourselves who we should be.

gets me through life with the least amount of difficulty or personal vulnerability.

I once made out a humorous listing of some of the more common acts or roles. The names are, I think, self-explanatory. This is my list (I'll bet you can add some):

Shirley Smiles
Mickey "Everybody's Buddy" Mascot
Peppermint Patty the People Pleaser
Dennis Doormat
Elsie Enabler
Elmer Egghead
Polly Porcupine
Henry Helper
Susie Shyness
Nathan Niceguy
Priscilla Peace-at-any-price
Milton Mindgames
Felicia Femme-fatale
Max Macho
I. M. Incredible
Gertie Gossip
Harry Humorist
Doris Dingbat
Freddy Fragile
Wilma Wimp
Matthew Muscles
Fanny Fashionplate

Even if you didn't see yourself anywhere on this list, I think we can reasonably presume that you and I have some kind of act going. Whatever it is, this act usually becomes an obstacle to self-honesty and good communication. Because my act is usually rehearsed each day, I gradually lose contact with who I really am. I can't easily tell where my act ends and the real me begins.

With regard to communication, I edit my self-disclosure and admit only to those thoughts-feelings-motives that are compatible with my act. For example: Some of us, like Wilma Wimp, choose weakness as an act so that others will carry us through life. Doris Dingbat will never be honest about her ability to make decisions or to take on difficult tasks. Freddy Fragile will not communicate anything about the core of toughness that he in fact possesses. He won't reveal his strength so he will never be called upon to use it. After a while even Freddy will lose touch with his hidden powers.

My own (John) act was to be a helper. I usually tried to make that clear right from the start in every relationship. "I am the helper. You are the helpee." I also bridged over into enabling: doing things for others, making decisions for them, enabling them to remain weak. I didn't challenge those who came to me to grow their own muscles, to make their own decisions, to act against their crippling fears. I spoke up for them, acted as a proxy for them, told them what I would do if I were in their place. Of course, the payoff for being a helper is the consolation of the gratitude expressed by the whole clientele of dependent people. Helpers actually feel good about helping others. In fact, helpers aid and abet infantile dependency, but they don't have to face this because so many people are ready to thank them for their efforts.

When it comes to communication, helpers are like everybody else who has an "act" on the stage. They edit their communication, never admitting their own need for help. They pose as "having it all together" because otherwise someone might try to help them. That would blow their cover. Sometime I would like to write a book entitled *Confessions of a Former Helper*. Such a posture does have its exhausting aspects. Those of us who have tried to play Messiah know that it is difficult to have an answer for every question, a solution for every problem. House calls and night visits become routine. However, to give up the role would seem almost like losing one's identity. Also the "dependent clientele" strongly insists that the Messiah stay up on Mount Olympus. They have a sense that "God is on my side" when they can seek counsel and get direction from the self-appointed guru, the helper.

Painted into this corner, I could never admit that I was afraid or that my feelings were hurt. I could never confess that I was just as puzzled by the situation as the questioner. Feelings of weakness, inadequacy, and human fallibility seemed very threatening. I could not say "no" to any appeal for help. It was "keep the role at any cost."

The tragedy is that no one ever got to know the real me, not even myself. I could not have had a true relationship because true relationships demand equality. The helper cannot allow this. It would ruin everything.

And I (Loretta) chose the role of enabler. I assumed a personal responsibility for every situation. It was the dependable, reliable me who always made things work out, who always rose above the emotionality and chaos. I took on the task of restoring order, clarity, and peace to all situations in which these had been lost. And when all my efforts still did not bring a positive resolution, I would assume the responsibility for that, too, thinking, "I must have made a mistake or maybe I did not do enough."

As an enabler I had to be good at long-suffering. There was no limit to the burdens I was willing to carry. I became the world's biggest and strongest bushel basket, so that I could catch and carry all available problems. I thought of myself as having limitless endurance. Of course the more problems I took on, the more life became a burden. But believe it or not, that's what made me feel satisfied with myself. I was "paying my dues."

As long as I insisted on being the enabler, everyone else in fact turned out to be a loser. Others lost the opportunity to bear their own burdens, to develop their own strengths, to become responsible for themselves and their lives. Of course, I was a loser, too. I had to settle for the apparent reward of being acclaimed as a "superresponsible person." Maintaining this position kept me so preoccupied that it was impossible to care for myself adequately. My personal growth process was put on "hold" so I could maintain the short-term recognition as an enabler. I could not care for myself, could not listen to my own needs or feelings. I even had to deny my true feelings. As a result I slowly but surely lost touch with myself. There was no real me to be offered to others as a gift. There was only the role. The real me got lost somewhere inside the role. Only now am I getting to know her.

Being honest with oneself requires giving up these acts and roles of ours. But prior to the surrender must come the recognition. What is my act? It has been said that all of us carry a sign out in front of ourselves. We have composed it ourselves; it announces us. We get treated accordingly. If the sign reads "Dingbat," others do not come to us for serious conversation. And if our sign reads "Doormat," others will tend to roll right over us.

The curious thing about our signs is that others can read them quite clearly, even though we are often unaware of our own self-advertisements. This, I think, is one of our more common fears of intimacy. If I let you get close to me, you will see through my act; you will expose my charade. It could leave me feeling utterly naked.

So once more the question boomerangs back to me: Do I really believe that I must be honest with myself in order to be authentic with you? Do I really want to be honest with myself? Do I really want to be honest with you? Do I want to share my true gift with you, or do I want to play it safe and give you only my charade? My act is the price I pay for my safety and my strokes. It is the armor that protects me from getting hurt, but it is also a barrier within myself that stunts my growth. Likewise it is a wall between us that will prevent you from getting to know the real me. Giving up my act will take much courage. I will be taking a real risk, walking out from behind my wall. I will have to rewrite my sign: "This is the real me. What you see is what you get." Be patient with me. This will not be easy. I suspect that old Polonius knew this when he advised Laertes: "To thine own self be true."

However, if I am willing to take this risk, my courage will reap magnificent rewards: the statue will come to life. I will get to know who I really am. Maybe for the first time I will realize where the role ends and the real me begins. The real me will emerge from behind the mask, the sham, the pretense. I will begin to thrive in my relationships and grow into the best possible me. The ancient Greeks knew all this when they accepted as the summary of all wisdom: "Know thyself."

The longest journey is the journey inward. *Bon Voyage!*

Guidelines for the Successful Practice of Sharing Oneself (Speaking)

4

In sharing ourselves with others, we must always take full responsibility for our own actions and reactions. As a consequence of this, we will make "I statements," not "You statements."

Most of us grew up as "blamers." We accused others of making us angry. We rationalized many of our reactions by telling others, "You had it coming." Or we insisted that they had provoked our response. "I just couldn't help it." "I would have been all right if she hadn't started it." It is difficult for most of us to look back and acknowledge that our actions and reactions were not caused by others but rather by something in us. Yet this is always the fact. If I can only cross over the line that separates the blamers from those who accept the full responsibility for their behavior, it will probably be the most mature thing I have ever done. At least it will bring me into an honest contact with reality, and this is the only way to grow into a mature human being.

To illustrate this truth of personal responsibility, I have often suggested a hypothetical situation to my classes. "If someone in this class suddenly stomped out of the room, angry and insisting that he or she would never come back, would never listen to me again, how do you suppose I would react? What do you think I would do? How would I feel?"

A variety of answers is usually forthcoming. "Oh, you would be *angry*. You would shake your head and your fist. You would get that person's name and number and threaten retaliation. You would say, 'You're not going to get away with this.' "

Someone else usually suggests, "No, I think you would feel *hurt*. You would get a crushed look on your face, and you would ask sadly, 'How could you do this to me? I was doing the best I could.' "

Still another member of the class often comes back, "I would imagine that you would react by feeling *guilty*. You would wonder what you had done to provoke such a hostile reaction. You would probably ask the others in the class, 'What did I do?' Or you might run after the departing person, and apologize. You would ask that person to come back, to give you another chance."

I am always a bit relieved when another student insists that I would feel *compassion*. "You would feel sorry for the person

Most of us grew up as "blamers."
If I can only cross over the line
that separates the blamers from those who accept
the full responsibility for their behavior,
it will probably be the most mature thing
I have ever done.

and probably think: It's too bad he is so tightly wired. He's probably not ready for this yet."

And so on and so on. There is an almost infinite number of possible reactions: "Rejection . . . depression . . . anxiety . . . compassion . . . fear . . . feeling like a failure," and so forth.

I'm always glad to have such a wide variety of responses because this enables me to point out that any one of the suggested reactions is possible. But please notice: The reaction will not be determined by the person walking out, but rather by something in myself. I also know that another person in my place would probably have a different reaction than I would. What determines my emotional and behavioral reactions is in fact my own attitudes or personal perspective. If I perceive myself as good and the matter I am teaching as important, I would probably react with compassion. If I perceive myself to be a klutz that always has footprints around his mouth, I would probably react apologetically. If my attitudes and perspective are paranoid, I would be sure that "that kid is out to get me."

Very often it is difficult to find, beneath a reaction, the attitudes and perspective that explain the reaction. However, that is a different problem, and one that is not directly pertinent to our point of personal responsibility. What is pertinent is the inner admission that whatever my reaction is, it is not caused by the stimulating agent but by something in myself. You may have heard of the sign that the late Eleanor Roosevelt kept posted on the wall of her office: "No one can make you feel inferior, unless you give him permission." In fact, no one can *make* us feel or act in any certain way. Something *in us* always remains in charge of our emotional and behavioral reactions. Other persons, circumstances, or situations may stimulate a reaction. We determine what that reaction will be.

The opposite to owning one's own reactions is blaming or, to use the more technical word, *projection.* Projection is a standard and commonly used defense mechanism. When I project, I blame someone else or something else for my failures or undesirable reactions. I do not take personal responsibility for my reactions but lay that responsibility on another person. Obviously, communication becomes nothing more than a game if it is not honest, and projection is simply not honest.

As we have said, another person or circumstance may stimulate a reaction in me. But the specific way that I react will be determined by my own attitudes and personal perspective. These in turn have been shaped by the messages recorded on my mind-tapes and the experiences of my life. Attitudes are as highly personal as fingerprints. Consequently, no two people ever see anything in exactly the same way, and so no two people ever react in exactly the same way. You may laugh off something that I will take seriously. You may react compassionately to a person with whom I would become angry. Let us suppose that the very same thing happens to both of us. It is very possible that you will be exhilarated by the challenge while I am devastated by the catastrophe.

A blamer who projects the responsibility for his or her reactions never really grows up. The life of such a person is a perpetual exercise in projection and rationalization. It is a life of pretense that is never penetrated by reality. Blamers insist that someone else is pulling their strings. So they never really get to know the inner reality of themselves. "The fault, Dear Brutus, is not with our stars but within ourselves that we are underlings" (*Julius Caesar,* Act 1, Scene 2).

If we really sit and soak in the truth of all this, it will be immediately apparent in our communication. We will make

"I statements" rather than "You statements." The significance of this will be far greater than a mere choice of words.

Let us suppose that I have reacted angrily to something you have done or said. In this case I can tell you of my anger in one of two ways: (1) "You made me angry!" (This is a "You statement.") (2) Or I can say, "When you said what you did, I felt angry." (This is an "I statement.") The first expression, the "You statement," directly denies the truth of all that we have said about personal responsibility for our own reactions. But more than this, it lays a guilt trip on you. It is an attempted but thinly disguised manipulation. I am maneuvering you into the position of the "bad guy." Right? Such a remark, if you are the combative type, will invite you into a heated, win-lose argument. It will certainly generate more heat than light.

However, if I make an "I statement"—"I felt angry"—I am assuming responsibility for my own reaction. I am acknowledging that another person in my position might well have reacted differently. I may not easily or readily understand all the attitudes and the perspective that have shaped my reaction. However, I do know that my reaction has been the result of something in me. When I make an "I statement," I admit this to myself and to you.

In fact, I notice that I get angry at some people while others only feel sorry for them. I get upset by certain circumstances while others take them in stride. I perceive some situations as "absolutely awful," but I am aware that others see these exact situations as "a chance to be creative."

The important personal effect of all this is that if I do own my own reactions and accept responsibility for them, I will discover my true self. I will gradually realize that I do have some crippling, distorted attitudes that must be revised. And this kind of honesty will prove to be an irresistible initiation into maturity. I will hear myself saying things like: "I act like such a baby when things don't go my way." I will have to be honest and tell you, "When you yawned during our conversation, I interpreted this as disinterest and I felt sad and sorry for myself." If I continue this openness and honesty of "I statements," I will grow up and we will really be communicating.

It may be that right now you and I are trapped in a quicksand of projection and blaming. It may be that we have never truly known ourselves because we have always looked outside ourselves for an understanding of our persons and our reactions. If we can change this thinking, the results will be very rewarding. We will get to know ourselves as we really are and we will find ourselves involved in true sharing rather than in the deception of blaming.

And honesty, it is said, is always the best policy.

5

We must speak only for ourselves. In communicating I should make it clear that I am speaking only my *truth, and not* the *truth.*

Most of us are tempted to generalize our personal experience. We forget that others are really other, different from us. We often make the false presumption that everyone reacts exactly as we do. And so in describing our own personal reactions, we say things like this: "I was stopped on the street today by a roving reporter. She asked me what I thought about our new mayor. I started babbling before I gave myself a chance to think. You know how it is. You know, you get overeager and enthusiastic, and then you throw open the motor of your mouth before your mind has had a chance to warm up. Then you notice that your foot is implanted in your mouth. You know that you've done it again. Right?"

Wrong! Even though I can personally identify with most of this experience, there are many more calculating people who simply would not recognize themselves or their tendencies in such a description. There are even some zipper-lipped types who don't ever say very much, even when their minds are whirring. I can speak for myself, but certainly not for them. In fact, I can speak only for myself. I am an expert only on myself. When I project my own reactions into others, this often results in a difficult situation. I impose upon my listener the embarrassing burden of saying, "Oh, no, I don't react that way at all." At which time the person who insists on speaking for everyone will probably smile serenely and say, "Oh, you say you don't but actually, if you were in my situation, you would react the same way." And that's when most people silently ask themselves, "What can I say?"

The temptation to generalize is an indication that I have discovered "otherness" only imperfectly. I have not yet fully realized how unique and individual each of us is. Because of this I am still tempted to project my reactions into others. If something hurts or bothers me, I presume that it will hurt or bother everyone. If a given situation stimulates a worried reaction in me, I presume that anyone would worry in such a situation. Such a habit of thinking and speaking makes me the norm of all human reality. Do you remember the cartoon character named General Bullmoose? His motto was: "Whatever is good for Bullmoose is good for the nation." He was a man who thought and spoke for everyone.

Actually, we human beings do have much in common, but we are never less than individuals. The way we react to things, even things like beauty and humor, will be different in each of us. In other words, I can tell you only my experience, my reaction. And you can tell me only yours. Neither of us can presume to know the intricate workings of each other's mind and heart. Much less can we presume that our minds and hearts will work in exactly the same way.

The person who has realized our individuality and uniqueness will not only speak more carefully and only for self, but will ask before assuming. I remember once watching a person doing a task in a way that I thought was very time consuming. My own game with life is to "build better mousetraps," to devise new and creative ways to do everyday tasks. I asked the person I was watching, "Would you like to know an easier way to do that?" Presuming that the answer would be "yes," I started to move in. My friend developed a posture of resistance: "Did it ever occur to you that I am enjoying this method and am not looking for an easier way to do it?" Zonk. A new application of the lesson of "otherness."

There is a serious consequence of this human individuality when we are discussing what is true and what is false. In our courts of law, witnesses are asked to "tell the truth, the whole truth, and nothing but the truth." But witnesses are asked to testify only about that which they have personally seen and heard. It is presumed that no one witness knows the whole truth. I think that all of us acknowledge this in theory. It is much harder for most of us to practice our acknowledgment. We fall into the trap of attributing infallibility to our observations, our interpretations, the way we remember it. We lapse into frequent communication failures as a result.

We say things like this: "You said this. You did. I remember it clearly." If I were speaking *my truth* and not *the truth,* I would probably say something like: "It seems to me that you said this or that. At least that's the way I remember hearing it. Did you really say it, or is my memory deceiving me?" It would certainly lubricate good communication and promote a pleasant exchange if we were to speak in this way.

Very often we find ourselves involved in a difference of opinion. It would be speaking only *my truth* and an attractive invitation to communication if I were to say, "This is the way I see it ..." Or we might say, "I have always been under the impression that ..." People who think that they can speak *the truth* tend to pontificate: "This is the way it is. It was this way in the beginning, is now and ever shall be." This kind of arrogance is for most of us an invitation to contradiction, not to communication.

No human being on the face of this earth possesses the whole truth. Each of us has only a small part; but if we are willing to share our small parts, our pieces of the truth, we will all possess a much fuller reality, a much larger share of the total truth.

The picture comes to mind of two people on opposite sides of a solid fence. One side of the fence is painted brown and the other green. If the person on the green side keeps insisting, "This fence definitely is green," he will invite contradiction from the person standing on the other side of the fence. "No it's not. It's clearly brown." Obviously, each has a part of the truth, just as we all do in most of our

No human being on the face of this earth possesses the whole truth. Each of us has only a small part; but if we are willing to share our small parts, our pieces of the truth, we will all possess a much fuller reality, a much larger share of the total truth.

disagreements. It's hard to imagine that a person could be totally wrong about any complex issue. Everyone has some part of the truth to share.

It makes sense, doesn't it? Well then, where do we so often go wrong? Sometimes I think that the issues we discuss and debate are never isolated from a larger context. In most human relationships there are unseen "scorecards." A woman who is starved for affection or affirmation may well bring up an issue of disagreement just to let off some of her bottled-up steam. A man who thinks that his ego has been dented or diminished may well do the same.

Someone has wisely said that most of us do not argue about the real issues. Rather, we displace our feelings and tie them to phony issues. A husband complains about how much his wife has spent for her new shoes, and she in turn reminds him that he has not fixed the screen door as promised. But the price of the shoes and the screen door are not what is really bothering them. In such circumstances, a personal triumph seems more desirable than truth. So we wind up setting the record straight on the unseen scorecard. We win an imagined victory by knocking over straw men, and telling others the truth, the whole truth, and nothing but the truth!

How foolish of me to pretend that I have the whole truth when in fact I have only one small piece!

6

We must share all our significant feelings with those to whom we are relating.

We human beings are not simple. There are very many intricate parts in us. We have sense perceptions, which our minds organize into ideas. Our wills exercise the power of choice. And, oh yes, both mind and body produce our emotions. Of course, it is true that these feelings or emotions are not the most important parts of us. They come and they go, sometimes in opposite directions. They are affected by the amount of sleep we have had, the time of day, the "sugar level" of our blood, and sometimes by the barometer. But in the act of communication, in sharing ourselves with others, they are the heart of the matter. Why?

I'm fairly sure that when you or I confide our *feelings* to another, we have a sense that we are really sharing our *true selves.* We don't have many completely original thoughts. At least I can't remember having one. And we haven't made many original choices. But no one in all of human history has had your precise feelings. No one has ever felt as I do. Our feelings are as unique and original as our fingerprints. For example, a person might summarize himself or herself by saying, "I am a Christian and a lawyer, and my family is my life." Nice and neat. But you don't really get to know the individual person from such summary statements. The majority of Americans identify with Christianity, and there is a lawyer for every seven thousand of us. Devotees of the family are also fairly common.

People who are willing to share only their thoughts and choices with us in this manner might as well be sharing the last book they have read. But if a person confides and describes his or her feelings—the loneliness and the struggling, the fears and the joys, the peace of certainty and the pain of doubt—then we will have a sense that we are getting to know who the person really is. Tell me what you think and I can possibly put you in a category; tell me what you feel and I will get to know you.

Our feelings in a sense are the summary expressions of our whole personal history. They are not simply our own highly personalized reaction to a given person or situation. They grow out of our earliest human experiences, our so-called "parent tapes" (messages received from parents and other significant persons early in life). Also, we model our emotional reactions on those of our parents, our brothers and sisters. But our emotional reactions are never exact copies because they are also an expression of our own unique human experiences. They capsulize the times we were bullied or humiliated by youthful antagonists. They incorporate and talk about the security or insecurity of our childhood homes and schools and neighborhoods. In fact, they summarize and express all the roots of our highly individual human existence.

Viewed only in a here-and-now context, our emotions are the psychophysical reactions to our perceptions. If I perceive you to be my friend, I will feel secure when I am with you. The perception comes first. The emotion results from the perception. Historically, our perceptions, the way we see or perceive a given object, have been largely shaped by other significant persons and events in our lives. These persons and events are like recorded messages that have been left on our mind-machines.

Consequently, in telling you my feelings I am somehow sharing with you my whole life: the people who have influenced me, the experiences that have shaped me. It is true that my feelings can be tilted in one direction or another by recent amounts of sleep or food, by what has gone right or wrong during my day. Still the sharing of my feelings is my ultimate self-revelation. In confiding my feelings to you, I may be saying that a person who has had my parents and experiences reacts thus and so when he is tired or hungry. I am always telling you where I have been and who I am when I am sharing my feelings with you.

In the full act of sharing myself with you, I cannot just drop my emotions at your feet. How puzzling it would be if I just informed you, "I'm furious!" If you are to understand, I must offer you a context of full self-awareness. Of course, this presumes that I have been working at self-awareness, listening to the things that are going on inside me. The full context of self-awareness would go something like this:

(1) I first give you the *data of my senses.* "I saw and heard you laughing when I was giving my serious presentation before the delegates to our convention."

(2) I then give you *my tentative interpretation of this sense data.* (Please note that these interpretations must always be presented as *tentative.* A tentative interpretation is the way I am subjectively and for the time being interpreting what I saw and heard.) "I interpreted that you regarded my thoughts as silly or stupid. At least, I thought that you were not giving me the support of serious listening. I thought that you were my friend, but there you were laughing at me. Those were my inner thoughts when I saw and heard you laughing. Of course, I could be ten miles from the truth, and maybe I was taking myself a little too seriously, but that's the interpretation I made." Notice that a tentative interpretation also gives you a chance to help me revise my interpretation, if it needs revision. However, if I can't tell you of my tentative interpretation, I will go on thinking the worst and you will never know what is bothering me.

(3) Next, I give you *the feelings that resulted in me from my interpretation*. "And so I felt angry with you. But anger is often only the top emotion covering layers and layers of other feelings. As best I can dig them out, I felt 'deserted' by you, my good friend. *'Et tu, Brute?'* It was the old shock of Julius Caesar, who was sad and surprised that his good friend, Brutus, would be among his attackers. Real dramatic, eh?"

(4) Finally, wherever possible I add *additional context* for my reaction. "You know, that was the first time I had ever made a presentation at any convention. It was my debut as a speaker and so I got all wrapped up in myself. Instead of thinking about the audience, I was thinking only about myself. I kept wondering how I was doing. It's also true that I was so nervous about that darned speech that I hadn't been sleeping or eating too well. Please don't think that you have to agree or disagree with me or even explain anything. I'm not really trying to make a point or challenge you. I just want to share my inner self with you. I hope you will be able to accept me. Anyway, thanks very much for listening to all this."

By the way, in sharing all our significant feelings, it is extremely important to share our "positive" or "affirming" feelings as well as our "negative" feelings. In the dialogue above, the speaker could well have said, "When I looked out and saw you and noticed your close attention to everything I was saying, I felt secure and confident. In fact, every time I felt the panic of 'What am I doing up here?' I looked at you. Thanks so much for being a good friend at a time when I really needed a good friend." More than anything else, people need our *affirming* emotional reactions.

We have already discussed motivation for communication. The difficult thing about discussing motivation is that our motivation is often "hidden." Sometimes we try to disguise or deny our true motivation, not only from others but even from ourselves. Almost all of us have at some time had the experience of someone assuring us, "I'm only telling you this for your own good." Then we got laid out in lavender, because it was allegedly "for our own good."

The point here is this: My motive can be either *ventilation, manipulation,* or *communication.* If I tell you my feelings because I want to *ventilate,* I am not sharing myself as a gift to be given, but I am using you as a garbage dump for my emotional refuse, so that I can feel better (and you feel worse, most probably). If my motive is *manipulation,* I am consciously or subconsciously maneuvering you. I may want you to feel responsible for me and my emotions, to feel guilty for having caused my emotions, or even to give me the sympathy I am seeking. Again, this is not a gift being given, but only a ploy. Although we may try to disguise or deny such motives, they will eventually show through and cause pain, like the thorns on a rosebush.

The only acceptable motive for sharing my feelings is *communication.* I tell you my feelings because I want you to know the real me, and I want to have a real relationship with you, not an "arrangement" mistakenly called "friendship." I know from personal experience that I have felt the urge to tell others my feelings in order to get even, to punish them, to extract an apology. All these are unacceptable motives. They are not fair. They tend to destroy, not to build up, a personal relationship.

Consequently, I may have to include in the fuller context of my sharing the admission that these feelings are roaming around in me, that I feel an urge to get even with you for my real or supposed grievances and hurts, that I want you to apologize for your oversight. Along with my other shared material, I include an explanation of this, such as:

I hope that these are not the hidden agenda of my sharing. I trust that they are not a concealed motive for this sharing.

Somewhere back in quieter times of reflection I have realized that the only way to a deep and real relationship is to tell you all my significant feelings. I really want this. I want our relationship to be deep and real. Although I am emotionally stretched between ambivalent feelings, I trust that my real motive is one of caring and sharing.

This, then, becomes a complete communication. It is a full, open, honest sharing of my real self with you. All I can hope for is that you will listen and take my sharing into gentle hands.

To share or not to share . . . a few examples

So often people pose as being close, but never really get to know each other because they keep their emotions hidden under the clichés of argumentation. I remember a couple coming to me, both angrily protesting that divorce was the only way to solve their problems. Honestly, they would not even look at each other. It seems that he had been arrested and she felt so humiliated that she couldn't live with the thought that it might happen again. I invited both to sit down and try an experiment with me. "I want you to tell me your feelings about this incompatibility you are experiencing. Just

*I have realized that the only way
to a deep and real relationship
is to tell you all my significant feelings.
All I can hope for is that you will listen
and take my sharing into gentle hands.*

feelings now. No accusations. No recital of past failures. No judgments. Just feelings." I began with the woman because I had seen her once previously and thought that the chances of success were better with her.

In response to my invitation, she described her central emotion as "insecurity." "I really don't know what to do or where to turn. I can't understand the situation we're in so I don't know what to do about it. I just want to run away and leave it all behind. But this means divorce, and then I start feeling 'guilty.' I was brought up to believe in the sacredness of the marriage commitment. I remember saying in my marriage vows, '. . . for better or for worse.'" After she had described her sense of guilt, she seemed to discover in her cascading emotions another strain of feelings. "I think I feel 'responsible' for him. It's like I am his mother as well as his wife. I have felt compelled to instruct, shield, and defend him. I make excuses for him and have even lied to spare him. Whenever I think about my role as 'his protector,' I get a 'burdened' feeling, as though I have been carrying a heavy weight on my shoulders."

The wife did well. But there seemed to be an obvious omission and so I had to ask her. "You didn't mention anger, and yet, when you came into my office, you looked angry. You looked as though you wanted to hurt him. Were you feeling this way?" "Oh, no," she sobbed. "He has been hurt enough. No, I'm not angry, just really sorry for him because he has gone through a lot." By this time the poor husband's eyes were like saucers. I am quite sure he had not dreamed that these were the unexpressed feelings of his wife.

Then I turned to him, and he did almost as well as his wife. His central feeling was "shame." "Sometimes I feel as though I should be wearing a sign 'Leper!' or something. I sometimes imagine that the whole human race is having a picnic and I didn't get invited. I get very 'lonely' and sometimes when our children are sitting on my lap, a fear comes over me that I may infect them with my weaknesses and that they will have to go through the same kind of hell I am living in." With occasional encouragement, he continued on through various layers of feeling, and ended with this surprise:

"This last feeling is hard for me to say. Because I am a big man, and have always wanted to appear masculine, I never thought anyone would ever understand this feeling. (Long pause ...) I feel like a little boy who wants to cry but who needs permission. I need someone to say, 'It's okay to cry. You'll still be a man.'" With this his wife moved out of her chair and cradled his head in her arms. "It's okay, Honey," she whispered, "you can cry. I'll always love you." After a few tears, he stood up and embraced her. "Thanks. I think I needed that," he said softly.

It is true that I have condensed an hour into several paragraphs, but I think it is an accurate summary. I have always had a secret wish that I could have and show a videotape of that meeting. It would illustrate so clearly what a true exchange of feelings can do to a relationship. By the way, I don't know if my friends have "lived happily ever after." I do know that they are still together "for better or for worse." And somehow I am confident that they are really getting to know each other.

I (John) also have memories of my own family of origin. Whenever we argued, it was usually a pointless dialogue of the deaf, a series of win-lose contests. There was no exchange of feelings as an act of sharing. My father was a very good man. However, he was totally unwilling or unable to share his inner feelings. He had verbal defenses always ready: "I keep my own counsel." "Never mind!" "Keep your bowels open and your mouth shut, I always say." And so he died, with all his secrets locked inside himself and now forever locked in his coffin. My mother and I were with him when he died. After I gently placed his head back on the pillow and closed his eyes, I told my mother that the struggle was over, that Dad was dead. Her first instinctive reaction was to tell me, "Oh, John, he was so proud of you. He loved you very much." I wondered why she said that. Minutes later, however, as I was looking through the corridors of the hospital for a doctor to confirm my father's death, the reason for her remarks became clear to me. She knew that he had never said these things. My father never told me he was proud of me or that he loved me.

Before my father's death I did not understand or appreciate the value of emotional openness. When I did become aware that a deep human relationship is impossible without such openness, I was determined to get to know my mother. In the long hours of her declining years we spent much time confiding our feelings to each other. When she died, it was so much different from the dying of my father. I was filled with a sense of fullness rather than emptiness. My tears were saying, "She was a truly beautiful person. I am so glad that I got to know her."

However, I live with the regret that very possibly my mother and father never really got to know each other. I am afraid that if an angel were to write the appropriate epitaph on the single stone that marks their place of rest, it would read: "Here lie two very good and decent people who never really knew each other."

I also recall a time when a man confided to me that his son had been killed in a highway accident. He told me that he composed a note on the night before his son was buried and gently placed it under the boy's body. It read:

My Dear Son:

I never told you how much I loved you. I never told you what a large part of my heart you occupied. I never told you what an important role in my life you played. I thought that there would be a right time for this: when you graduated from school, when you would leave our home and set out on your own, when you got married. But now you are dead and there will never be a right time. So I am writing this note and hoping that God will tell one of his angels to read this to you. I want you to know of my love for you, and my sorrow that I never told you of that love.

Your Dad

I (Loretta) have found emotional openness to be particularly difficult in connection with death. I have had three major struggles with my feelings after the deaths of my father, my mother, and my grandmother. When I was three and a half years old, my father, a Chicago policeman, was shot and killed while on duty. My emotions of grief were pretty well hidden in my young heart. I repeatedly told myself, "It doesn't hurt." I followed the example of those around me without questioning. Without processing my sadness, anger, and grief, I accepted my dad's death as an act of God. From an act of God only good things should follow. Inside, however, I was troubled with many confused thoughts and ambivalent feelings for many years. I can still quote some of my inner conversations of those times:

Why did he have to go somewhere else to be happy? He was happy here with me.

I know he didn't want to leave me, but I sure see why he wanted to leave Mom. She is so sad, and all she does is work. She's no fun at all.

Why did he have to die and not her?

She never loved him as I did. It's all her fault.

How could he go and leave me here with her?

He's the only one who ever really understood me.

I don't think I ever did anything wrong to make him go . . . or did I? Maybe I really am bad, like everyone says I am when I am being stubborn.

I wouldn't be so stubborn and bad if he came back.

These inner dialogues with myself were never shared. I even denied within myself the emotions beneath them. I never spoke about my feelings of rejection, anger, resentment, fear, hurt, sadness, self-pity, guilt, and hope.

As I grew older I also grew to love and admire my mother. She died twenty-eight years after my father's death. By that time I was old enough and had learned enough to respect the free, open expression of emotions. Grieving for my mother was really a double grief. I was grieving for her but also for my father. It was a gigantic task. However, with the help of a few patient and empathic friends, I did do my "grief work" openly and completely. As a result, I think I grew very much from the experience.

Five years later my grandmother died. Grieving for my grandmother, a second mother to me, was very different. I was comfortable with the process. I knowingly entered into it and almost welcomed it. This third period of grieving provided added benefits. I shared my deepest feelings with my grandmother before she died. During and after her dying, other family members and I were comfortable enough to want to share our grief together. I had learned from the earlier experiences that emotional openness was healing if only I would let it happen freely. I became aware that unexpressed emotions do not disappear but continue to haunt a person until they are recognized and processed. I learned that I could get to know the specialness of others through the mutual sharing of our feelings. I would also get to know myself better. And I would grow as a person through the grieving process.

Finally, I would like to share with you another occasion in my life when I had a public (though peaceful) disagreement with a respected man, much older and more revered than myself. We had both made presentations at a convention. In my presentation I had been promoting total emotional openness in all close relationships. My friend felt compelled to disagree. "I could not tell my wife all my feelings," he admitted. "It would destroy her. So I edit my feelings. What I do tell her of my feelings is always true. But of course I do not tell her all my significant feelings." We peacefully agreed to disagree, to let the members of the audience decide for themselves.

Several years later, my friend left his wife. She wrote on her Christmas card to me: "He has decided to leave me and our home. He will soon marry another woman." Of course, I am too old to think that I have X-ray eyes and can see through people. Still, I often wonder if it wasn't what he did *not* tell his wife that destroyed his love for her.

At another, week-long convention I was at the speakers' table with a man named Charlie Shedd. Charlie kept reassuring the delegates that "my Martha will be coming on Wednesday." When his wife, Martha, arrived, he proudly escorted her to the platform. There he introduced and publicly embraced his bride of forty years. I kept mumbling to myself, "Love works. Look. Love really works." In a subsequent presentation at that gathering Charlie Shedd told us that when he and Martha had pronounced the traditional marriage vows, ". . . for richer or poorer, in sickness and in health, for better or for worse," they added privately a pack of ten promises. One of them was "total emotional openness within forty-eight hours." Charlie told us, "We added the rider about forty-eight hours in case I would come home with a throbbing emotion and Martha would have a throbbing headache. In that case my emotion could wait until her headache was gone."

"Love works!" I kept saying to myself. But apparently love works only for those who work at it. Love works for those who will take the less traveled road and run the risks of complete emotional openness. It is certainly true that my feelings are unique. They summarize and express my whole life experience and my unique person. If the true gift of love is the gift of myself through self-disclosure, then I must entrust my feelings to those I love.

And to those I love: Please take my feelings into careful hands. And when you hold them, remember that they are a very important part of me. Thank you.

7

We must be courageous enough to share our personal vulnerability with one another.

There is a theory about inferiority complexes which I am willing and ready to accept. This theory contends that we all have inferiority complexes. These complexes come almost as an inherited part of our infancy and early childhood. They are firmly established in the first five years of life. Someone who counts such things has written that the average child, during the first five years of life, receives 431 (!) negative messages on an average day. "Stop making that noise ... Get down from there ... What are you doing with my scissors? ... No, you're too small ... Look at the mess you've made ... You've got dirt on your shoes and I just cleaned the kitchen floor!" And so forth (× 431).

As a result of these negative messages, we develop instincts of self-protection. We try to cover or pad our egos to prevent further damage. Psychologists call these protective efforts "ego-defense mechanisms." The most common of these are the five described here:

(1) Through *compensation* we lean over backward to avoid falling on our faces. Freud calls it *reversal*, or *reaction formation*. For example, the dogmatic know-it-all keeps pontificating in order to repress the doubts that might arise in him or her and undermine the safety of being certain. The little boy "whistles in the dark" as he walks through a cemetery at night. The stubborn little girl keeps insisting, "It doesn't hurt ... It doesn't hurt!"

(2) By *displacement* we construct a psychological detour, an alternate course or outlet for impulses that we can't let out directly. For example, I can't express my hostility to my

boss whom I find obnoxious because I might get fired. So I go to a baseball game and yell, "Kill the umpire!" Or I put my fist through a wall, after kicking the cat. Another kind of displacement is expressing my true emotions but about the wrong issue. A woman who feels starved for affection may not be able to ask her husband to hold her, but she can complain that he is always late, or hasn't lifted a hand to help her clean out the basement.

(3) By what is called *projection,* we cleverly disown undesirable qualities in ourselves, but attribute these repugnant qualities to someone or something else. In projection, as noted earlier, we shift the responsibility for our shortcomings and failures from ourselves to someone or something else. You will remember that when God confronted Adam in the Garden of Eden, Adam blamed his failure on Eve. "This woman you gave me—she tempted me!" When God turns his question to Eve, she said it was all the snake's fault. "The snake tricked me into eating the forbidden fruit," says Eve. In other common projections we blame our poor work on inadequate tools. And some with an astrological inclination have even claimed that their failure was due to the fact that their "moon wasn't in the right house." Or perhaps, "The devil made me do it."

(4) Another method of ego-defense is called *introjection.* When we introject, we claim as our own the good qualities or deeds of others, sharing vicariously in their achievements and basking in the rays of their glory. It is also possible to introject a sense of persecution or personal martyrdom. We imagine ourselves as heroic victims. Also, it is a form of introjection when we identify our material possessions with our persons, and swell with pride when someone admires our mink coat or fancy yacht. There are many forms of introjection. We can identify with athletic or television heroes

or heroines. One Manhattan psychiatrist, Dr. Louis Berg, actually forbids his patients to watch the "soaps" because there are so few happy persons in them. The doctor fears that his patients will introject the sense of dramatic tragedy found in most of the characters.

(5) Finally, there is *rationalization.* I think it is the most prevalent and widely used of the ego-defenses. It is a phony exercise in self-justification. This self-deception can be worked in various ways. For example, I may find good reasons to excuse myself from doing what I know I should. Or I may find justification for doing what I know is wrong. If I fail to keep a promise to you, I rationalize that you didn't really think I was serious. Or if I find your wallet, I rationalize that Robin Hood became a hero by stealing from the rich to give to the poor! Sometimes the self-deception of rationalization seems to have no outer limits.

These are the most common cover-ups or ego-defense mechanisms. They are all impediments to good communication because they somehow conceal our vulnerability. The problem is that we do not really communicate our true selves when we are engaged in one of these ego-defenses. We are not being real. Consequently, we cannot grow up to our full potential. We will never fully mature as long as we indulge in these self-protective defenses because they are barriers to authenticity. In one way or another they keep us from contact with reality.

A healthy and growing person accepts the human condition of weakness. "People are mistake makers, and I am one of them. That's why they put erasers on pencils, you know." Healthy and growing persons are also good communicators because they are ready to share openly and honestly. They share not only the light and bright but also the weak and wounded side of themselves.

From our first discovery of language, we are tempted to use it *not* to express and reveal our true selves, but to pretend and to manipulate reality. As children we got rewarded for our self-proclaimed goodness. "I was a good boy all year. Honest, Santa Claus." We also learned how to use the manipulation of tears to get attention. Later in life the misuse of language can assume more serious proportions when we tell people that we love them in order to use them. And once used, these manipulated people become "trophies of conquest" and take their places in our trophy cases. And usually, the deception is planned and executed simply to prove that we are not really inferior. It is simply another cover-up of our vulnerability.

Obviously, these defenses of our wounded egos lead us into endless and sticky games of phoniness. Fortunately, there is a positive, creative, and health-producing antidote. It is simply to accept ourselves in the human condition of weakness and to admit the facts of our limitations. Such honesty and openness counteracts our unhealthy tendencies. Honesty and openness, willingness to share ourselves, warts and all, makes us real. It puts us into the kind of contact with reality that enables us to grow up and to become all that we can become.

I have a physician friend who once told me of a hidden desire. He said he would "someday like to stand on a high balcony above the world, and announce to the whole human race, 'THIS IS ME. THIS IS ALL OF ME. THERE IS NO MORE. THERE IS NO LESS. CAN YOU ACCEPT ME AS I AM OR NOT?' "

I told him that I knew what he meant. There is such a strong desire in most of us to shed our pretense, our sham, our phoniness. We all would like to be real. Phoniness requires so much effort. And once we start playing the game, we have to keep playing it. We would like to be able to put our real selves on the line (if not the balcony) rather than put an act on the stage. What a relief it would be to tell it like it truly is, to feel safe and secure in just being ourselves.

Such honesty would challenge us to stretch, to step out of our comfort zones. To tell our truth openly to everyone seems very frightening. The consequences of honesty sometimes seem too high a price. But not to worry. It takes about three weeks, according to the experts, to get in the groove of a new habit, if we practice it every day. The open admission of our human woundedness and weakness may well look like a mountain until we start the climbing. I know from personal experience that most of us anticipate the worst: "The world will stop spinning through space. The light of the sun will go out. I will probably faint. Others will gasp in disbelief." And these are our more mild anticipations. But none of this happens. In fact, we immediately experience and recognize in ourselves a new honesty and realness.

At the same time others sense and reflect back to us their recognition of our authenticity. Our relationships become real, grounded in an honest self-disclosure. We realize that most of our fears are often more tormenting than the actual experience. We do most of our suffering on the way to the dentist and not in his chair.

Opening up my weak and wounded side, my fears and immature habits, even my phoniness and pretenses, will be such a relief. Taking you into my "closed rooms" will be a freeing experience for me. And in the exchange of such communication, you will get to know the real me. Our communication will no longer offer you only an edited and abridged version of me. What you see will be what you get: the one and only, the real me.

You won't be afraid of me or be tempted to glorify me as someone who has it all together. You will know that I am a mistake maker and that I experience in myself the human condition of weakness. I personally like to tell people to whom I am relating, "If you ever get my number, it will certainly be a fraction. Part of me feels certain; part of me doubts. Part of me is loving; another part of me is selfish. Part of me is confident; part of me is insecure. Part of me is proud; another part is humble." I have gradually become more content with being such an ambivalent person, who seems to be split right down the middle.

The peace that comes with such self-disclosure is an immediate and undeniable reward. People who are willing to share their vulnerability don't have to keep up the exhausting effort of repression. They don't have to tie masks over their faces. They don't have to go through the contortions of compensation, projection, and rationalization. They make what Dag Hammarskjold called the "longest journey," the inward journey into self. What they see and hear in this exploration of their inner spaces they put out on the ticker tape of communication. "This is me. This is all of me, no more, no less. If you can come and celebrate it with me, fine. I must tell you this: I don't have to please you. What I have to do is be myself, my own true self."

Only when we are willing to share our whole selves, warts and all, are we really communicating. But more than this, my openness will have a definite effect on others. Honesty, like

We are as healthy and whole
as we are open and honest
with ourselves and with others.

everything else that is human, is contagious. My coming out from behind protective walls to meet you face-to-face will inspire you to do the same. When we are real and honest about our vulnerability, others are immediately relieved. They know that we have taken a risk in exposing our "warts and all" selves. By our honesty they are invited and encouraged to take off their masks, to reveal their own inner selves openly and honestly. They are empowered to take a similar risk, and they will experience a similar sense of freedom.

Just the other day a fine man came to visit me. He immediately made the honest admission that he is a "recovering alcoholic." He had been sober for several years and was going through the well-known "Twelve Steps" of Alcoholics Anonymous. He told me that he had already made the Fourth Step: ". . . a searching and fearless moral inventory" of himself. Now he wanted to move on to the Fifth Step: the admission of specific guilt.

Then, in a very open way, he confided that there "is something, a weakness in myself I have never told anyone. I was hoping that I could tell you." He fearlessly proceeded to open up his closed room, and we looked into it together. Actually what he shared with me did not seem to be an uncommon weakness. In my own wordy way I explained all I knew about the subject, hoping that the sharing of this background knowledge would prove comforting. Just before he left, I asked him if he did feel comforted and relieved. "Yes," he said. "What you told me was very helpful. But the main feeling of relief came with my own disclosure, just getting it out."

He left my office, and I do not know if I will ever see him again. But this is for sure: I will never forget him. He was honest and real. Honest and real people tend to have this effect on us.

I would not like to leave you with the impression that making a general confession of all our sins is a necessary part of good communication. The Fifth Step of Alcoholics Anonymous asks its members to admit "to God, to ourselves, and to *another human being* the exact nature of our wrongs." There may be some serious mistakes we have made which we would choose to confide only to a confessor or a very trusted friend. However, the kind of vulnerability of which we have been speaking here would include our fears, tendencies of weakness, everyday kind of mistakes, limitations, grudges, hurts, embarrassments, undesirable reactions, difficulties, shortcomings, and the pretenses that have become a part of us. And these should all be part of an ongoing communication if a good relationship is to grow better.

Finally, another bit of wisdom I have gained from an AA friend is: We are as sick as we are secret. On the other side of the coin is a positive expression of the same truth: We are as healthy and whole as we are open and honest with ourselves and with others.

Remember: The first three weeks are the hardest!

8

We should express gratitude to our listeners.

Communication is a free exchange of gifts. The speaker gives the gift of self through self-disclosure. The listener takes that gift into gentle, understanding hands. This response of the listener is itself a gift. It is such an encouraging and reassuring gift that some expression of gratitude is in order.

There is a well-substantiated theory called "the positive reinforcement of conduct." According to this theory, if a person is somehow rewarded or thanked for a certain behavior, he or she will tend to repeat that behavior. Unfortunately, we often ignore this rule of conduct. We too easily take things for granted. I take it for granted that when I am speaking, you will be listening. After all, I reason, it is only polite. So why should I be explicit in my gratitude? Wasn't it the least you could do?

The question, I think, overlooks the implications in the gift of listening. Let's analyze this gift of the true listener. When you listen to me, the first thing you must do is put your own life aside in order to give me the time I need. I know from personal experience that this is not always easy. By some mysterious inner drive I am geared to accomplish. As a result I always have a daily agenda, a clear listing of things that I want to do on a given day. When someone knocks at my door, my first impulse is to wonder, "Who is it now, and how long are you going to stay?" My mind is usually all wrapped around some project, and I have to loosen my mental tentacles one by one. My will is almost always set on finishing the project I am working on. My enthusiasm is usually running high. Then someone walks in and asks if I have some time. My visitor says that he or she is bothered by something and wonders if we can talk it over. Reluctantly, if willingly, I put aside my agenda

*Sometimes I think of it
in terms of physical space.
The listener clears a place in his or her life
for the speaker to move in, sit down,
and spread out the pieces of a personal puzzle.*

and redirect my mind, my will, and my enthusiasm to someone else's concerns and away from my own.

Perhaps this is a little dramatic, but every good listener does just this in some way for the speaker. The listener sets his or her own life aside and gives the speaker that which the speaker needs most: the encouragement of someone who cares. Sometimes I think of it in terms of physical space. The listener clears a place in his or her life for the speaker to move in, sit down, and spread out the pieces of a personal puzzle. The listener has to make room for the speaker.

A good listener is not just a sacrificial lamb, who goes through the motions of virtuous self-sacrifice. The good listener truly wants to know who the speaker is. Very often we complain, "Nobody really wants to listen to me and my problems. Nobody really cares." In fact, good listeners care enough to turn away from their own concerns, to ignore their own deadlines, and to direct all their attention to us and our concerns. They care enough to want to know who we are, and this is something for which we must all be explicitly grateful. "Thank you for turning away from your own needs and concerns. Thank you for wanting to know who I really am. It certainly made it much easier for me to share with you my own inner spaces."

Besides this gift a good listener gives me the freedom to be who I am. I am almost painfully aware that you are different from me. My thoughts are not your thoughts and your thoughts are not mine. My fears are not your fears. My worries may not find any resonant echoes inside you. The things that stir anger and resentment in me may well be the things you can take so easily in your stride. And yet you give me the freedom to be different: to fear what you do not fear, to worry about that which would not cause you worry, and to feel resentment for persons that you would only pity.

A good listener offers us even more than this acceptance of our differences. The good listener goes out to experience vicariously whatever we are trying to share. The good listener makes an effort to get inside us, to look out through our eyes, to feel our fears, to relive with us our reactions. The good listener just says, "Yes, of course," or "I see" and we immediately feel understood.

I am sure that you have at some time said to a listener as I have, "Oh, I don't expect or need you to agree with me. Just try to understand me and where I'm coming from." The good listener offers us this gift of empathy, which assures us that we are not alone. This gift of going out of self and somehow standing with us is a very precious gift. It would be a serious oversight to omit an expression of gratitude.

There is one other thing that an expression of gratitude accomplishes and clarifies. When I thank you for listening to me, I implicitly make it clear that this was all that I was asking of you. I was not inviting you to solve my problems for me. That would be immature on my part. I was not trying to manipulate you by some subtle accusation, or to put you on trial. I was not even challenging you to evaluate my sharing.

I was only asking you for the great gift of putting aside your own life and agendas for a while and sharing a personal concern with me. I was asking you for the gift of letting me be different from you. I was asking you for the gift of accepting me at the place I am right now. A simple word of gratitude says all this. It lets you know that I appreciate the many gifts involved in the gift of your listening. At the same time, my gratitude reminds me that you are not a thing to be used or a person to be taken for granted.

I remember a time in my own life when I felt a vague resentment toward my mother. I wasn't sure what the resentment really was, but I knew it was there. I was becoming impatient and inwardly critical of almost everything she said or did. I knew that there had to be some deeper, underlying resentment. Exploring the hidden roots of my feelings, I finally discovered the source of my resentment. And so I asked my mother if we could talk.

"Fine," she said, "I've been wanting to hear all about what you have been doing. I heard your name was in the newspaper." When we got comfortably situated in the kitchen, I summarized for her what I knew about the problem of semantics. We never hear with full accuracy what another person is saying. I belabored the point with a couple of examples. "I can tell one woman that she is 'sweet' and she will hear this as a compliment and will thank me. But I can tell another woman that she is 'sweet' and she will hear something unpleasant. To her 'sweet' may mean 'sticky, saccharine, and maudlin.' She will bristle at being called 'sweet.' "

A second example. "I can tell one boy not to play in the street, and he will know that I care. But it may be that if I tell his twin brother the very same thing, he will be sure that I don't like him or want him to have any fun." People never hear exactly what we are saying. And the important thing is not *what we say* but *what they hear*.

Mama said she understood all of this, but was wondering where it was leading. But first there was one more preliminary point to be made: "So I can never say to you, 'You said this!' but I can only say, 'This is what I heard you say.' Right?" Mother nodded her understanding and agreement.

So I was now ready to share with her something I had been hearing all my life: "If you love me and want to please me, be a big success. Make me proud of you." I underlined the fact that she may never have intended this or even implied it. It was only something I had been hearing. And the whole problem, I admitted, could well have been a matter of my hearing. I stressed that I was only sharing this with her so I wouldn't act it out in stupid and immature ways. When we don't speak out our resentments in clear communication, we do act them out. We give frosty looks, slam doors, and pout; and eventually we get ulcers. I didn't want to do this to my mother or myself.

I was on thin ice and knew it. Communication always has in it an element of risk. So I added another reassurance that I was not demanding a response. I was certainly not putting my mother on trial. I reassured her that I remembered a thousand acts of love and a thousand sandwiches wrapped in waxed paper and put into little brown bags for school. I remembered a thousand socks she darned, and another thousand happy moments sitting on her lap as she read to me. Then I also thanked her clearly and effusively for letting me say what I did. I thanked her for letting me sound ungrateful and for letting me tell her of my troubled feelings. And at the very end, I assured her that she had been a good listener. I also promised that if ever she had anything she wanted to share with me, I would come running. I would try to be the empathic listener. I would take her sharing into my own gentle, appreciative hands.

It was not just a ploy to get off the thin ice. It was a true expression of gratitude. Near the end of my mother's life a small incident made me realize that success was something she no doubt wanted more for me than for herself. Mother was in her eighties and could no longer see very well. Reading and even watching television were difficult. I told her about some "fan mail" I had been getting, and asked her if she would like me to bring some along on my next visit. I offered to read them to her. I remember clearly her tired response: "All right, if you want to. But please don't bring too many of them." I laughed all the way home. I was again grateful that once upon a time she had let me be me, that she had let me have my thoughts and feelings, and that she had accepted me for who I was at that time.

Very often when we are sharing our so-called "negative" feelings, without intending it we might make it sound like a trial, a challenge, a confrontation. "Thank you very much for letting me be me and for letting me tell you about it!" at the end puts things into perspective. It also supplies a context for our sharing that clarifies and classifies our self-disclosure as a gift of self. Our expression of gratitude makes it clear that this "gift" was not a thinly veiled accusation or a manipulation. It was simply a gift, no strings attached.

Oh, and thank you for listening.

PART THREE

Guidelines for the Successful Practice of Accepting the Sharing of Another (Listening)

9

We should be "present" and "available" to others who offer to share themselves with us.

All of us know what it means to be physically present to another. We can be distracted or dreaming, but as long as we are in the same room, we are physically present. However, we are not speaking of *physical* presence here, but rather of a *personal* presence. This personal presence implies much more than just being a warm body in the same room. I am personally present to you when I am giving you all my attention. Everything else for the moment has been shut out. The lenses of my mind are focused on you and on what you are sharing with me.

If we work up the courage to share ourselves with another and we suspect that this other person has something else on his or her mind, we will probably sense this. Or if the other person is registering boredom in manner and body language, we will lose all desire to place our fragile gift in such uncaring hands. It is difficult for a listener to fake true presence. Human intuition usually sees right through pretended presence. If you are wondering how long I will go on talking, I will somehow perceive this. If you have other things that you would rather be doing than listening to me, I will somehow realize this, too.

It is difficult for most of us to work up to real honesty and openness. Consequently, we need the atmosphere and support of true presence to attempt a profound sharing of ourselves. I don't want to take the obvious risks of self-disclosure if you look bored or distracted. I don't want to put a tender and sensitive part of myself in your hands only to watch you yawn or notice your attempt to change the subject. I don't want to share my joy or my success with you if you appear to be too preoccupied to celebrate with me.

"Availability" is a closely related concept. All of us know what it is like to knock on a door and get no response. We know what it is like to dial a phone number with a sense of urgency only to get a busy signal. There is a similar reaction of disappointment in most of us when we truly wish to share some profound part of ourselves only to notice that our supposed listener does not seem to be available. We sense that this other person would rather not be troubled with us and our sharing. When we get such a "busy signal," we usually just hang up. We are tempted to give up.

Early on Sunday morning, August 5, 1962, Marilyn Monroe was found dead. The coroner would later call it "suicide." When Marilyn's maid discovered her lifeless body on that Sunday morning, she noticed that the phone by her bedside was dangling off the hook. Marilyn had obviously made a last attempt to communicate with someone. When her last attempt failed, she gave up and died alone.

Clare Booth Luce wrote a very poignant article for *Life* magazine, entitled: "What Really Killed Marilyn." The subtitle read: "The 'Love Goddess' who never found any love." The author suggests that the dangling phone was an apt symbol for the whole of Marilyn's life. She tried for a long time to say that she was a person, but few ever took her seriously. Only after her death did many of the facts of her life surface.

Marilyn Monroe was seriously disliked by most of her Hollywood contemporaries. She was dubbed a "prima donna." Very often she would arrive hours late for a filming. As she casually strolled into the studio, no one suspected that she had been at her home nervously vomiting. She was terrified, afraid of cameras. No doubt her emotional reactions were the result of a sad and troubled childhood. Her father, an itinerant baker, had deserted the family. Her mother was repeatedly committed to mental institutions. Marilyn was raped at age eight by a boarder in her foster home. She was given a nickel not to tell.

Now, at age thirty-five, her mirror kept telling her that the only thing others ever noticed about or praised in her was fading. She must have felt like an artist who is losing his vision or a musician whose hands are becoming arthritic. Marilyn had endured a painful childhood, had moved through several marriages and made many movies; but few ever took her seriously . . . until she was dead.

Then the whole country did a national act of contrition. We asked Clare Booth Luce's question: What really killed Marilyn? Perhaps the dangling telephone says it all. No one cared enough to be present and available. Perhaps that phone thrown down in despair is a sad symbol of a tragic attempt to be heard. If the phone symbolizes Marilyn Monroe's frustration that ended in death, she is herself perhaps the

symbol of countless human beings who want to be heard, but
who have given up.

In his book *The Power of Compassion,* Father Jim
McNamara tells the story of one of these unheard human
beings who wandered off alone into the night. As I remember
the story, which Father McNamara tells about himself, it
occurred when the author was an assistant pastor in an eastern
city parish. The housekeeper told Father McNamara that a
young man waiting in the offices of the rectory wanted to see
a priest.

Jim McNamara walked slowly to the offices, reflecting that
he was not "on call" that day, and that it was almost supper
time. There in the office sat a young man. His clothes told the
priest that he was poor. He introduced himself only as "Jim."
As Jim began his story, he mentioned that he was out of work.
The priest could see it coming. He was going to ask for
money. Deep inside himself he was hoping that the
housekeeper would interrupt and call him to dinner. The sad
story of the young man dragged slowly on. Then the
housekeeper did knock on the office door to tell Father
McNamara that he was wanted on the telephone. He excused
himself to answer the phone call.

When he returned, Father McNamara found that Jim had
left. The priest sensed that his manner had revealed his
preoccupation with other things. So he looked outside, up
and down the street, but could not see his departed visitor.
Feeling the growing twinges of remorse, he got into his car
and drove through the neighborhood. Finally he spotted Jim
and pulled his car up to the curb. When he called out to the
young man, there was no answer. The poor fellow just kept
on walking. So the priest left his car, ran to the sidewalk, and
stood in front of the young man: "Jim, I'm sorry that I had to
leave. Would you come back with me and finish our

conversation?" The young man simply shrugged and said in a low whisper, "You're just like everybody else. No one wants to listen." With that Jim walked around the priest and disappeared into the night.

Being present and available to another human being is the infallible sign of love and caring. Every one of us that walks the face of this earth is looking for such a sign, but not daring to count on it. We are all braced for the signs of disinterest. When we see them, we sadly disappear into the darkness of the night.

Perhaps the most common obstacle to giving this presence and availability is our fixation on ourselves and our own concerns. I once asked a personal friend, who happens to be a psychiatrist, why it is so hard for us to get out of ourselves. My friend smiled at me and asked, "Did you ever have a toothache?" I replied, "Yes, I have." He countered with another question: "Who were you thinking about when your tooth was hurting?" I thought for only a short moment and replied, "Me! I was thinking of me." "Yes, indeed. And anyone else?" Again, after only a short reflection, "Oh yes, the dentist. Any dentist who could relieve me of my pain."

My psychiatrist friend seemed to think that the whole answer to my question was contained in my responses about the toothache. He pointed out that we are all hurting, and that pain has a way of magnetizing our attention to ourselves. At times we all have experienced physical pains, like a toothache, but almost continually we experience some feelings of inadequacy, inferiority, anxiety, and guilt. If we let these feelings attract all our attention, we will have little presence to offer others. We will have a neon sign on our foreheads, flashing: "Not Available."

In the Introduction to this book, we mentioned that no habit is ever achieved without practice. The habits of presence

and availability are not exceptions. An old American Indian saying reminds us that "to truly understand another human being, we must first walk a mile in his moccasins." To this we would like to add the suggestion that we cannot walk in another's moccasins unless we first take off our own. We have to make a real effort as listeners to get out of ourselves, to unshackle ourselves from our personal preoccupations, and to donate our presence and availability to others.

At first this will be very difficult, but as with every other human accomplishment, practice will make it easier and easier until it becomes habitual. Presence and availability are very valuable accomplishments, and certainly worth the effort of our repetition and practice. Those others trying to tell us their story, the Marilyns and the Jims, as well as our friends and family members, will be forever grateful to us.

So let's exchange our shoes and walk a mile together.

Pain has a way of magnetizing our attention
to ourselves. Almost continually
we experience some feelings of inadequacy,
inferiority, anxiety, and guilt.
If we let these feelings attract all our attention,
we will have little presence to offer others.
We will have a neon sign on our foreheads,
flashing: "Not Available."

10

We should accept others wherever they are.

Life itself is a process and we are all "beings in process." None of us has yet come to full maturity; none of us has arrived at completion. We are all fractions on our way to becoming whole numbers. I remember once seeing this sign on a button a woman was wearing: "Please be patient. God is not finished with me yet." God is not finished with any of us yet. We are all en route to our full personal growth and potential. And certainly we all need a lot of patience during the process— patience from ourselves and patience from others.

In the recent research on death and dying, it has emerged that the dying person usually goes through five stages on the way to the peaceful acceptance of death. These stages could be characterized as:

1. Denial (No, not me!)
2. Anger (Dammit! Why me?)
3. Bargaining (Yes me, but what if . . . ?)
4. Depressed Resignation (Yes, I am going to die, but I feel very sad about having to leave this world.)
5. Peaceful Acceptance (My work is done. I am ready now to go through the door of death.)

Death and dying counselors warn us that this gradual movement toward a peaceful acceptance of death is a process. They caution us that if we try to move the dying from the stage where they actually are to the stage where we would like them to be, we will probably shut down the whole process. People have to be allowed to move through the dying process at their own pace. True acceptance of a dying person implies that we also accept the pace and the feelings of that person at each stage.

One such counselor tells the story of a dying woman who asked her, "Is there a screaming room in this hospital?" The counselor calmly replied, "No, but there is a chapel where you can pray." The dying person exploded. "If I had wanted to pray, I would have asked for the chapel. I want to scream!" She was obviously in the second stage, and the counselor admitted to the mistake of trying to move her away from her anger. The counselor was uncomfortable with the anger and would have preferred a peaceful acceptance. When we try to accelerate the process, it is often because we mistakenly think it will be helpful. Also, when someone has moved into a peaceful acceptance, it is much easier for us to deal with that person.

The process of human development and growth is much like this process of accepting death. We humans have to move at our own pace, and all during the process we need to be accepted wherever we are. We know, for example, that we cannot insist on consistently mature behavior from small children. We must let them be children and we must accept them as such. We also know that we cannot demand a rigid conformity from adolescents who are trying to learn how to think for themselves and become their own independent persons.

Actually, from conception to death each of us is involved in a continually spiraling process of change and growth: birth-death-new birth in all the phases of our personhood. Every stage of life has in it certain developmental tasks. To accomplish each task and so to further our personal development we must constantly be involved in changing. Obviously, changing always involves giving up the old and comfortable behaviors in order to embrace new and more mature behaviors.

There is a death and a birth in every change. And each death, however small or great, seems to require that we go through the five stages of dying before we can accept and experience new life. If those who love us will only accept us "in process," that will be the greatest gift of their love to us. The journey through life has many valleys that we just can't skip over, and also many mountains to climb that we just can't jump over. It is also true that we need the space and the freedom to make our own mistakes. Trial and error seem to be the only way we can learn and grow. Life is first and foremost a process. And this process is a zigzag process at that.

Consequently, there are no more intolerable tyrants than those who demand that we march to their drums, that we conform to their ideas for us. Sometimes such keepers of the collective conscience seem to be willing to accept us only if we are at a place designated by them. They do not seem willing to accept us in the human condition of process, which always involves trial and error. They have no patience with us "mistake makers." Like an army drill sergeant, they will accept only: "Yes, Yessir!"

All of us have some idea about how frightening self-disclosure can be. Sometimes it feels as though we are crawling out from behind old walls that have hidden and protected us. It feels as though we are ripping off the masks and shedding the roles that have been our only defense. We hold out in trembling hands the gift of our openness and honesty. We are hoping that our self-disclosure will be accepted gently and appreciatively. Of course, we try not to let our insecurity show. While waiting for the signs of acceptance we may even affect a casual, I-don't-care nonchalance. But deep inside we are holding our breath, and crossing our fingers.

When someone refuses to accept us where we are in the great life process, it is as though such a person is saying to us, "I do not accept you or your gift. I had something else in mind, something different, something better and more advanced than you are. I cannot possibly approve or accept you as you are."

Of course, we don't make speeches like this to one another. When we do not accept another wherever that person happens to be, we simply look impatient and disappointed. Then we leap in with unasked advice, which is usually overloaded with suggestions for change and improvement. It is obvious that we accept only what the other person can become, not what that person actually is right now. As Charlie Brown once moaned, "The greatest burden in life is to have a great potential."

Why do we find it so hard to accept others at their place in the life process? Why do we try to move them to a place where we would prefer to find them? I'm sure that different people have different reasons. However, one that probably motivates most of us is this: We fear self-complacency in others. I reason that if I accept you where you are, you may just want to stay there. You will become self-satisfied. You will not seek to improve yourself. Somehow this temptation seems to make logical sense, but the human, psychological truth is quite different. The human truth is that, faced with nonacceptance and disapproval, you and I are much more likely to stay fixed in a stagnant place. We will have little desire or strength for self-improvement and growth. We are somehow stripped of our strength if others continue to show disappointment and constantly offer advice about changing us.

What we might be overlooking is the fact that every person has a natural, built-in tendency to grow. Personal growth is something like physical growth. When we look at the body of a small child, we know that all the child needs is time and the proper nourishment. In time the small child's body will grow into its full development. Likewise, when we find another human being somewhere in the course of his or her personal process and progress, we have to have faith that with time and the proper nourishment that person will grow into full maturity.

The proper nourishment for personal growth is a loving acceptance and encouragement by others, not rejection and impatient suggestions for improvement. Human beings, like plants, grow in the soil of acceptance, not in the atmosphere of rejection. We have said that personal growth resembles physical growth: all the energies and tendencies are there. But there is in most of us a civil war that stunts our personal growth. It is our inner struggle for self-acceptance.

The noise and clamor, the push and pull between self-acceptance and self-rejection, produce the emotional parasites that drain off all our energies. These lost energies were designed to promote and produce growth. Every one of us experiences some struggle with inner anxiety, insecurity, fears of inadequacy, and feelings of inferiority and guilt. These negative forces increase in fury when we are criticized and rejected by others. And the stronger they become, the more

*Human beings, like plants,
grow in the soil of acceptance,
not in the atmosphere of rejection.*

painful the civil war becomes. The vision of our ideals is clouded by the dust of this inner conflict. The psychic energies that were meant to be directed to the pursuit of growth are wilted in the heat of the interior struggle.

We are all affected by this human condition of insecurity. Whenever we try to open ourselves up, no matter how nonchalant we pretend to be about it, deep within ourselves we are scared. Every effort to be totally honest and open seems to have a frightening price. What we need most of all is a gentle and reassuring acceptance. We need someone to assure us that it is all right for us to be whoever and wherever we are.

When we detect signs that our listener is closing us out, when we detect the signs of impatience and disappointment, the civil war of our inner fears heats up. The demons of insecurity and inferiority that haunt us begin to move in for the kill. Aware of our dangerous position, we will probably choose prudence as the better part of valor. We will slowly crawl back behind our walls of protection. We will find our discarded masks and decide that it is safer to wear them. It will seem better to pretend rather than to run the risk of being real.

On the other hand, if you will accept me wherever I am, all my energies and desires to grow will be released. If you will reassure me that it is all right to be where I am now, I will have the courage to move beyond where I am. But I will also begin to learn that I can be authentic in my communication without being punished for my openness or rejected for my honesty.

I (John) teach theology in a university setting. It is not at all unusual on this scene that the students should challenge the validity of religious faith. For years I yielded to the temptation to argue, to persuade, to refute, and to counterbalance the doubts expressed by students with my own sense of certainty. When I was finally struck by the insight that this was a form of nonacceptance, and contrary to everything I truly believe, I couldn't wait for the next occasion. When it came, the old and standard objections sounded mild. They were presented in a manner that was somewhat quizzical rather than bitter and belligerent. A tall, handsome kid remarked that he didn't experience God in his life, and that he wondered about others who said they did. Maybe they did, he conceded, but maybe they just had overheated imaginations.

I almost jumped at the chance. "Hey, Joe, that's really honest of you. Thanks for sharing yourself so openly with the rest of us. You know where I am, Joe. I'm up here talking about it all the time. Obviously you are not where I am, and that's good. You're not supposed to be where I am. But I would like to know where you are. I would like to go to your place and walk along with you for a while."

And so, right there in the classroom, Joe spun out his whole story of doubts and certainties, then doubts about his doubts, and so forth. At the conclusion of his story, I again thanked him. I tried to say as clearly as I could that I thought it was good for him to be where he was, and that I accepted him there. I also mentioned that I remember being in a similar place when I was his age. "You're asking thoughtful questions, Joe, and that is good. You're being honest about your doubts, and that is good, too. In fact, Joe, you're a pretty good guy. I hope you know that."

It proved to be the beginning of a long and treasured friendship. In the course of our subsequent sharing with each other, we have both moved far beyond where we were on that day in the classroom. And I think that part of our progress is due to the fact that he knows I accept him wherever he is, and he in turn lets me be me.

One last word on the subject. We have been discussing the importance of accepting others wherever they are. Our context has been that of communication. It is obvious that there are times when parents will have to discipline their growing children. They will have to forbid certain destructive behaviors. They will have to love their kids with what has been called "tough love." Also, there are times in the course of mature friendships when we have to challenge our friends in a loving way. Challenge is certainly a valid part of true love. There are likewise situations that call for us to confront those we love. For example, if a friend or family member is becoming chemically dependent, true love demands confrontation. We can't sit comfortably in our box seats watching those we love destroy themselves.

But the discipline, the tough love, the challenge, and the confrontation will all backfire if they are not built on the foundation of acceptance. At certain times in all our relationships we will need to balance an occasional nonacceptance of behavior with a clear and continued acceptance of the person. It is always absolutely essential that we accept the other person wherever he or she is in the great process of becoming a mature human being.

So whoever and wherever you are in your life process: We accept and love you!

11

We must listen attentively to learn the "inner consistency" of others.

Since communication is a sharing between two or more persons, it implies a good transmitter or speaker; but communication also requires a good receiver or listener. It is very reassuring for us human beings to feel heard and understood. The really good listener does more than just understand the "content" of the sharing. He or she also listens for the "context" of the sharing.

Very often we fail at this deeper kind of listening. For example, you might say to me, "Everyone is always picking on me. They're out to get me." I will almost certainly think that your statement is an exaggeration. I will tend to think of you as a bit paranoid. If I think that merely hearing words is listening, I might repeat back to you what I have heard: "So I hear you saying that you feel that everyone is against you, right?" I might then feel satisfied that I have listened to you. I have grasped the content but not the context of your sharing. Understanding only the content is not enough.

There is something much more important that I can do. I can keep listening and keep encouraging you to share further until I have the context behind your seemingly exaggerated statement. I can take a walk in your moccasins for a mile. I can clothe myself with your skin, try on your mind, look through your eyes. Objectively, of course, you are probably wrong in your statement about everyone being out to get you. Most people probably are not even thinking about you, let alone out to get you. However, if I had been born to and raised by your parents, if I had been a member of your family, and if I had had all your childhood experiences and grown

up in your neighborhood, if I had seen all these things through your eyes—then indeed I would understand why you think and feel what you do. I would then begin to grasp the "inner consistency" of your thoughts and feelings. I might even conclude that if I were you, I would probably think and feel the same way.

A willingness to learn must be added to a willingness to listen. For most of us this is quite difficult. It asks me to leave where I am, and to go where you are. It even requires that I leave (not give up) my own convictions in order to experience yours. No doubt, if I reflect back to you not only my empathy but also my understanding of your "inner consistency," you will certainly be very grateful. You will feel understood. And this kind of listening in order to learn is a much more valuable gift than listening only long enough to prepare my responses.

Carl Rogers, the well-known psychologist-counselor, has compared us average human beings to a person who has slipped and fallen into a deep, dry well. He describes the feeling of desperation that the trapped person experiences, the agony of frustration that he or she cannot climb out of the well. This person who is imprisoned keeps knocking on the sides of the well with bruised and bleeding fists. KNOCK . . . KNOCK . . . KNOCK. After a while, it all seems so futile.

The really good listener does more than
just understand the "content" of the sharing.
He or she also listens for the "context"
of the sharing.

But the only alternative is to die, and be discovered someday as a set of blanched bones at the bottom of an abandoned well. So the trapped victim continues to knock. Then, finally, there is a responding knock from the outer side of the well. Knock ... knock ... knock. There is an explosion of joy and an enormous sense of relief in the poor, exhausted prisoner of the well. He or she realizes, "Someone knows I am here. Oh, thank God, someone knows that I am here."

Rogers suggests that most of us are much like this person trapped in the well. We feel the same sense of aloneness and futility. We know the desperation, the frustration of being trapped and alone. But the only alternative is to die alone and unnoticed. So we keep trying. We keep pounding our bruised and bleeding fists against the walls of the private worlds that keep us imprisoned.

And then someone really listens. This good listener not only hears our call for help (our message) but assures us that we (our persons) are understood. The good listener not only understands *what* we are saying but also *why* we are thinking and feeling as we do. When we realize this, there is an explosion of joy and a deep sense of relief: "Finally, someone knows that I am here. Someone knows what I have been going through. Oh, thank God, someone finally knows what it is like to be me."

As Somerset Maugham has said, each of us is a mysterious composite of our places, influences, and personal experiences. To use a technological analogy, we are something like a computer. Millions of messages have been fed into and recorded in our brains and nervous systems. Every muscle, fiber, and brain cell of our being has recorded and stored these countless messages. To complicate things further, we have an "unconscious mind," a storehouse of unacknowledged data by which we are constantly being influenced. In fact, if we were to stand an average human being next to the most sophisticated computer, the human being would prove to be far more intricate and complicated.

Sometimes I have thought of this "listening and learning" which we are talking about as comparable to looking for the undiscovered pieces of a jigsaw puzzle. The first installment of self-disclosure by another is often meaningless by itself. One piece of a puzzle does not make much sense of itself. But then will come another piece, if my listening is sensitive and my empathy is real. Slowly, one by one, the pieces will appear and fall together. The picture gradually begins to come clear. Of course, we never totally understand anyone, ourselves included. But we can gain a real sense of what it is like to be "other." We can understand something of the "inner consistency" of the thoughts and feelings of another human being. When this kind of understanding is offered to us, it is a mountaintop moment of consolation. "Thank God, someone finally knows what it is like to be me." The person who has truly been heard and understood will probably be permanently transformed by this magnificent gift.

Most of us, when we are in the listener's role, feel compelled to be speakers. We feel a compulsive inner urgency to interrupt others as soon as they start to reveal themselves. We feel a strange obligation to advise them, and to support our advice with a few chapters from our autobiographies. We jump in at the first pause, and go on nonstop unless we are exhausted and the other person is near despair. Regrettably, I have done this to others. I have also had this done to me. I have experienced the sadness of not being heard because someone has not cared enough to listen to my sharing and to learn who I really am.

For example, I have tried to share with others a persistent problem in my own recent life. It is a feeling of being "overextended." I get about twenty letters each day and almost as many phone calls. There is either a request or an invitation in most of them. Sometimes I think I should have been twins, but since the other fella never showed up, I am left to do my best with what I've got, which is one person and twenty-four hours a day. I have to say "No, I'm sorry!" to many sincere people with good causes. Since this problem is such a deep part of the fabric of my daily life, I have tried frequently to share it with others. Most of my listeners are good, sincere, and well intentioned. However, many of their responses have not been very helpful. I have concluded that a really good listener is sometimes hard to find. In my experience there are three types of nonlisteners.

The first type assures me that I don't really have a problem. They remind me that it would be much more painful to live a life of neglect, to be unwanted and uninvited. Sometimes I think of the experience this way: I am telling them about my having no shoes, and they are responding by telling me that there are others who have no feet. There are worse problems than mine. Of course I know this. But somehow I come away from this first type of nonlistener feeling sorry I ever brought the matter up. These people mean well, but they obviously don't want me to be where I am. They tell me where I should be, what I should be thinking, and how I should be feeling. (Their conclusion: If I had my head screwed on straight, I would realize that I have no problem.)

The second type (which unfortunately I tend to be when I am in the role of listener) is anxious to make a problem of the speaker's sharing and then solve it. When I have mentioned my own dilemma to this second type, they know immediately what I should do. "Listen, you get yourself a secretary with bad breath and the gentleness of a steelworker. I mean, one who has the tact of a sledgehammer. People who know they will have to deal with her will wind up drawing straws, with the loser making the call." Again, I presume that the sympathy is real and the intention is kind. But I want to protest: "I didn't want you to solve my problem. I just wanted you to hear it. I wanted you to hear *me*." I know that people grow up by solving their own problems, not by submitting them to others for suggested solutions. Sometimes it just isn't all that easy to get heard. Is it?

The third type of nonlistener tunes in only long enough to prime their own pump. Then they become "Old Faccful," giving you their own experiences starting at the turn of the century (or so it sometimes seems). "Yes, of course, I remember having that very problem. Lemme see now, it was about 1959 ..." The date is important only because the frustrated speaker knows that he or she will now suffer through a survey course in the personal history of the listener who does not really listen.

In the listening of human communication, it is not recommended that you minimize my sharing by putting things into perspective for me. Also it would not be helpful to cut off my sharing with a little well-placed advice. And please know that I did not intend my sharing to be an introduction to your personal history. But of this I can assure you: If you will listen long enough, you will eventually get enough of the pieces of my puzzle to know me. You will learn what it is like to be me. And I will be forever grateful for this favor. I will experience an explosion of joy! "Thank you for your time, your patience, and your perseverance. Thank you for wanting to know who I really am and what it is like to be me. Your patient listening and your awareness have assured me that I have been found. I will know that I am not alone here at the bottom of this well."

So please listen for the content and the context of my sharing, and I will thank God that someone knows what it is like to be me!

12

We must not indulge in mind reading by judging the intentions and motives of others.

In our Introduction it was suggested that imagination or fantasy takes over where honest and open communication leaves off. Mind reading and judging the hidden intentions of others is a work of imagination. Usually it is a destructive work. Such use of the imagination almost always misleads us, taking us into blind alleys. I know that every single time I have tried to mind read or to judge another's intentions, I have been wrong. Sometimes I have been wrong by inches but most of the time I have been wrong by miles.

I blush to remember the first time I was giving a series of inspiration-type talks to young people. During my very first presentation, there was a young man in the second row, who continually moaned and groaned, gasped and grimaced. I tried several seventy-five pound looks, but nothing daunted him. At the end of the talk, I asked my young audience to remain in the conference room in order to reflect on the things I had been saying. All but one did. Yes, you're right, the kid who was affecting exasperation climbed over the others in his row and followed me out of the room.

For a while I was afraid I might be sending out lethal rays and that the boy would be electrocuted. Then he put a heavy hand on my shoulder, and spun me around. "What is it?" I asked, wearing my seventy-five pound look.

"I'm really sorry," he said, "but I am going to be sick!" (Translate: throw up or vomit.) "Oh!" I said with sincere surprise in my voice. So we went together to an appropriate place and he was appropriately sick. Afterward I went to his room with him to make sure he would be all right. (Someone once told me that appendicitis can begin with nausea.)

He was a very nervous young man. He admitted that he always "tossed his cookies whenever they transport the troops." I asked if he was sick even before the talk that evening. He told me about getting sick on the bus earlier in the afternoon. "Why did you come to the talk?" I asked quite sympathetically. "Oh, because I thought you might give us the theme for the whole series of talks, and I didn't want to miss it." "Were you sick during the talk?" "Wow," he said with his hands over his face, "I was so sick I thought I might just lose it all right there in the conference room."

Repentant, I still had to satisfy another curiosity: "If you felt so sick during the talk, why didn't you just get up and leave?" "Oh," he said, with an air of puzzlement that I didn't get something was so obvious, "because that would have disturbed you." It was dark in the room, and I don't think he saw me blush. As I was leaving his room, content that he was going to make it through the night, his last words were: "Thanks for being so kind." After I closed the door and was alone in the corridor, I muttered to myself, "If he only knew what kind . . ."

As we have mentioned, people are very complicated. They are so "other," so different from us that we cannot safely project our thoughts, feelings, or motives into them. We cannot read their interiors by looking at their exteriors. Once the two of us (Loretta and John) gave a workshop over a period of three days in Australia. Under our breath we murmured to each other about the "man about five rows back, right in the middle." His face was stark and expressionless. He didn't even smile at our best jokes. We agreed that he was neither enjoying nor profiting from our talks and exercises. At the conclusion, however, he came up to us. He identified himself by name and occupation (he was a doctor). Then he actually started to cry while assuring us that our presentations had opened many new doors for him. He hoped he could share some of these insights with those he loved. After he turned to leave, we looked at each other with open mouths and saucer eyes. "You can't judge a book by its cover, can you?" Sometimes by inches, more often by miles.

Earlier we referred to the sadness and suicide of Marilyn Monroe. Her whole life story, as it was put together after her death, was a fabric of misunderstanding and false judgments. She had been seriously disliked by most of Hollywood. One director vowed to have nothing to do with her after they made one picture together. He moaned that "she has breasts of granite, and a brain of blue cheese." None of those unhappy and critical people suspected the emptiness and pain in the heart of the prima donna. Sometimes I wonder whether many of the glamorous people who smile for our cameras are also smiling on the inside.

Do we make the same kinds of mistakes about those who are close to us, about those with whom we have lived or worked? Would it be just as presumptuous and foolish to read the intentions or motives of someone we know well? Surprisingly, perhaps, the answer is a quite clear "yes." Just as Kramer didn't seem to know Kramer very well, so most of us are really strangers even to those who are closest to us. When we presume to know them, we overlook the element of human mystery. After reading only the introduction, we think we know the whole story. But there are many other chapters, the contents of which we couldn't even begin to guess.

When we were reviewing the standard defense mechanisms, we described what is called "reaction formation." It is a form of compensation for those thoughts, feelings, and supposed weaknesses that we don't want to admit. The boy who is frightened by the darkness of the night "whistles in the dark." Most of us don't want to wear our weaknesses and limitations where everyone can see them. So we keep them repressed by affecting misleading airs. When we can't live comfortably in the gray areas of doubt, we see everything as black and white. If we can't admit our buried angers, we become excessively sweet. And please note that these procedures are unconscious. We deceive even ourselves! Now since all of us do this, trying to read the minds of others is extremely foolish and presumptuous.

All of us engage in "reaction formation" to some extent. For example, most males probably worry about what they construe as cowardice in themselves. So they try to appear "macho" and tough. Many women are programmed not to admit envy, so they do not indulge in envy. They simply diminish the competition with a condescending type of criticism. But these are only isolated examples. Most of us are not secure enough to acknowledge and express our fears and weaknesses. Our inner problems usually result in exterior compensations. We affect phony qualities and engage in abrasive behavior. Most people let us play our games, but every once in a while some volunteer mind reader offers to look right through us. In the end we know that he or she is just as wrong about us as we are about others when we play the mind-reading game.

I hope you can coax out of your memory one instance in which you thought you had correctly read the motives and intentions of another, and then discovered that the hidden reality was quite different. I hope you have been shocked and surprised, for example, to find under a wreath of smiles an empty loneliness. I hope you have found out from personal experience just how mysterious we human beings can be. Just one such discovery can give us pause. Our mistaken judgments make us reevaluate our ability to read minds and judge intentions.

I remember someone who appeared confident to the point of arrogance. He was consistently disliked by most. Then one day I heard him admit, "I don't expect success whenever I do something. I only hope that my failures won't hurt other people." Every time I am tempted to see through someone, I recall my surprise at that admission.

I also remember a good-looking young woman telling me that she felt ugly because when she was little, she was seriously overweight. Other children called her names and made fun of her. Even after adolescence, she still identified mentally with that obese little girl who was the object of so much ridicule. It is very difficult to get unhooked from our past and to deal with ourselves as we are now, isn't it?

This is one reason that those in the same family don't really get to know one another. We all have a tendency to relate to our family members of the past. Youngest children remain

We tend to get people's "numbers"
very early in life.
We put them into neat classifications.

mothers' "babies" in the eyes of other family members. Or older children just don't want to admit that a younger brother or sister has grown up and is now an equal. And, perhaps the most common of all, we expect other family members to make the same life choices that we do. We tend to get people's "numbers" very early in life. We put them into neat classifications. We refuse to reclassify them. We can't get unhooked from our own pasts, and we won't let others get unhooked from our memories of them. And, of course, this is especially true in the case of those who are closest to us.

Sometimes by inches but mostly by miles. I have been wrong every time I have tried to read minds and judge intentions. And so I have concluded that the only way to know what someone is thinking or intending is simply to ask that person. Obviously we are all somewhat deceived about ourselves, and so what another would tell us in answer to our questions may not always be accurate or even truthful. But it sure beats our best guesses. Furthermore, asking always promotes an exchange of communication. Just as surely mind reading and judging tend to break down the lines of communication and separate people.

So the next time we feel confident, we should check out our assumptions. Human beings are simply too complicated and too different for guesswork. If you think someone has intended a remark sarcastically, ask. "Do you really mean that?" You may well find out it was a poorly aimed joke. The next time you are sure someone does not like you, feel free to ask. "Say, I read you as feeling uncomfortable with me. Am I reading you rightly, or is it just my imagination?" I am sure that the full explanation will involve some zigs and zags you did not anticipate. I remember having a student in my class who made no secret of her dislike for me. And so I asked her about it. "Have I embarrassed you or treated you unfairly?"

"No," she replied, "it's your confidence and obvious joy that gets me. You walk into class and you look so happy and so friendly that I can't stand it. You see, I'm very introverted, and simply saying 'hello' to someone requires a heroic effort on my part. I guess I hate you for making it look so easy." I stood there with my mouth open for a long, silent minute. Finally the word came out: "Really?"

Sometimes by inches and sometimes by miles, but there is always a surprise waiting for us in the inner truth of another! Here's hoping you like surprises.

13

We should register empathic and reassuring reactions to others when they are sharing themselves with us.

In one of the humorous scenes from the movie *Rocky I,* Adrian, the shy girl friend of the "Italian Stallion," retreats behind a closed door. Rocky knocks several times on the door, but there is no answer. Finally, he says in his own inimitable way, "Ya know, I ain't used to talkin' to a door." But there is still no answer.

Sometimes when I attempt the painful process of opening up and there is no reassuring response, I feel like using Rocky's line. The feeling that we are talking to a door is always uncomfortable and discouraging. It is a real turnoff. What we really want is an empathic reaction, a reassurance that we have been heard and that the listener has joined us in our experience.

Empathy has often been contrasted to *sympathy* and *neutrality*. By *sympathy* we share the emotional responses of another. We join that person especially in his or her suffering. There is always the danger, when we offer our sympathy, of seeming to be superior and patronizing. We reflect our aversion for this patronizing sympathy when we insist that we "don't want to be pitied." *Neutrality* is more like the closed door. Neutrality says, "I really don't care." This kind of indifference is very painful for most of us.

By *empathy* we share more totally in another's experience: the thoughts, feelings, and attitudes of that person. By empathy we put ourselves in somebody else's shoes. Through the powers of our minds and imaginations we think that person's thoughts, we want what that person is seeking, we feel whatever he or she is feeling. In short, we experience what that person is experiencing.

When we read a story or watch a movie, we usually empathize instinctively. We identify with the characters, going through their experiences vicariously. Even if the story or the movie is fiction, the characters become real for us. We vividly identify with them. Our hearts beat faster, our hair stands on end, and we run with them the whole gamut of human thoughts and feelings. In a sense we take on their persons. We somehow become them through this process of empathy. Sometimes we even want the "bad guys" to get away because we identify with them. We think of them as victims even though they are really being pursued by the "good guys."

Empathy, like the other skills involved in communication, is an ability that can be developed. Sometimes I think that the main obstacle to empathy is our persistent belief that everybody is exactly like us. We insistently believe that everyone sees things the way we do. Everyone reacts, we think, just as we do. To develop our powers of empathy we have to acknowledge the unique otherness of every human being. We must be able to leave our own frame of reference and our own instincts and take on those of another. In a sense, empathy is the basic skill of the listener in the communication process.

Empathy is difficult, as suggested, because of our human differences. It is especially difficult when someone disagrees with us or actually doesn't like us or something we are doing. To get out of our own shoes and put on theirs at moments like this is the perfection of empathy. One does not climb this mountain without a lot of previous experience with smaller hills. Empathy, like most skills, is acquired with only a gradual success.

Counselors are warned that often the least important thing about the self-disclosure of another is the words they use. In an effort to develop our ability to empathize we should attend to the verbal messages of others. But even more important are the nonverbal signals. These would include facial expressions, voice inflections and tones, pauses, and body language in general. It is not an easy thing to walk a mile in the moccasins of another. However, if we really want to get inside another's thoughts and attitudes and enter into his or her total experience, we can do it. The first, necessary step is to get out of our own moccasins.

Sometimes we offer another only our heads. It is relatively easy to listen only with the head. We carefully examine the facts presented and the logic involved. The head-only listener can easily leave the sharer feeling like a case or a problem. However, in hearing only the facts, we hear only a part and lose the whole. Usually the head-only listener is detoured from true empathy by hearing only literal words. "That's exactly what you said," he reminds us. However, words rarely mean the same thing to different people. Speakers and teachers are

often reminded: Don't hear only the question. Hear the questioner.

Another obstacle to empathy arises from the fact that we humans usually think much faster than we are able to talk. Consequently, a listener has to work at concentrating on the sharer. Since we think faster than the sharer can speak, little mental side trips can be a real temptation. If we succumb to the temptation, the sharer will probably notice this, and may conclude that we are bored or indifferent.

The most serious obstacle to empathy, however, is fixation with ourselves. We tend to relate what we are hearing to our own experiences. We make ourselves and our experiences the norm for everyone. "That's strange," we muse to ourselves, when hearing something we have never experienced. "Maybe this guy's elevator ought to be checked. I don't think it goes up to the top floor." Or we have an agenda of "things to be done" and wonder how long the speaker will continue to delay us from completing our agenda. In some way this impatience will show through our pretended interest. The speaker will usually read our sign clearly: "Sorry. You have not been classified as a Very Important Person."

I remember one night when I received a phone call from a troubled young man, whose voice quavered as he asked, "Can I come in to see you tonight?" Fortunately I picked up the distress and anxiety in the voice, and immediately invited him to "come on over right now." When he came into my office, he did not sit down, but paced back and forth nervously.

Sometimes I think that the main obstacle
to empathy is our persistent belief
that everybody is exactly like us.

He told me of his extreme anxiety as he was dialing the telephone in an attempt to reach me. He said that he kept repeating the question: "What if he isn't in?" Since this young man had attempted suicide several times, I presumed that he felt death stalking him and closing in. He needed help and he needed it now. I also knew that the source of his distress was his homosexual tendency.

After he worked off some of his initial nervousness by the pacing, I asked him to sit down. I began: "Frank, I am not homosexual, and I have never felt suicidal. But I have often wondered what it is like. I suppose it is a different experience for different people, but I really want to know what it is like for you. What is it like to be you? Can you help me understand? When you get up in the morning and look in the mirror, what is your reaction to what you see?"

It was not a counseling ploy. I really did want to know who my young friend was and what he was going through. And apparently the few questions I asked were all that he needed to get started. With occasional encouragement from me in the form of another question, he talked for an hour. He graphically described his loneliness, his painful relationship with his family, his feeling of being abandoned and alone. He talked about hating himself, and told me very vividly of a self-contempt that was eating away at him like a cancer. In a sense it was like reading a captivating novel or watching an engrossing but tragic movie. I was able, at least on that occasion, to leave where I was and get inside a very troubled person whose experiences have been very different from mine. I must have grunted emphatically a hundred times.

At the end, my young friend stood up and smiled. I remember his words: "You know, when I came in here I felt like Humpty Dumpty, completely broken, fragmented into a thousand pieces. I said to myself, 'All the king's horses and all the king's men can't possibly put me back together again.' But, you know something . . . I feel whole again. I really don't understand it, but it feels good to be whole again." He shook my hand warmly and left smiling.

Then I sat down, closed my eyes, and reflected on the experience. I think I went down into valleys that night and up on mountaintops where I had never been before. And I think I learned a lot about the healing power of empathy. It has been said that we never go out of the house and return home the same person because we are changed by our experiences. I am sure that it is equally true that we never go out of ourselves, to live briefly in the person and world of another, and return to our own lives as the same person. The healing and transformation of empathy is always mutual: it heals and transforms both the receiver and the giver.

For me the invitation to empathy begins with this question: What is it like to be you? And if I am really asking this question in relating to another, that other will hear my question as a statement of concern: "I care." Whether we are mourning or celebrating, it is difficult for us humans to be alone. An empathic reaction on the part of another is consoling and reassuring. It says in a clear and undeniable way, "You are not alone. I am with you because I care."

It sure beats talking to a door.

14

We should clarify the message that is being delivered, trying always to understand accurately the meaning of others.

When I ask someone to listen to me, I am seeking to make a connection. I want to connect in some way with another human being. Sometimes I simply want an exchange of pleasant, playful banter. In other situations I may want to bring about some kind of change. Maybe I want to persuade you to do something or to accept something. And there are times when the connection is one of a shared reflection when you and I join our minds in exploring some topic. There are many possible intentions I might have for connecting with you. Perhaps the most important of these communication connections are those in which I ask you simply to understand me. I need you to listen so you can enter my world and know who I really am. When this connection is made and I sense that you have understood me—that you know what it is like to be me—then I no longer feel alone.

Let's turn it around and suppose that I am listening to you in an attentive and accepting way. I resist mind reading, trying only to imagine what it is like to be you. However, even with these good intentions and efforts I am still not sure that I understand. I'm not sure that I really know what you are trying to share. I don't want to bridge this gap by guessing or assuming that I know what you mean. That could be dangerous. I want to be sure I really understand you and your meaning. And I want you to be assured that I really do understand. So what do I do?

In this case, I have to work to clarify your message. There are three types of clarification. Each of these types deals with a different level of understanding. The first of these types is simply: *Asking for more information.* If the message I am receiving seems indirect or incomplete, I have to look for and locate whatever might be missing. The second type of clarification is: *Checking out word meanings.* It may be a matter of word usage. The meanings you attach to your words may be quite different from those I understand. In this case I must ask you to share your definitions with me.

Finally, the third type of clarification we might call: *Verifying my understanding of your experience.* In this case the content and word meanings may be clear, but somehow I am not sure that I have really understood the whole tone or emotional impact of your experience. In this case I reflect back to you your sharing as I have understood it to make sure that I have really grasped the impact of your experience on you. I will have to ask you to help me understand the dimensions of the experience that I may have missed. In each of the three types of clarification, a good listener is simply trying to make sure that the meaning of the speaker has been accurately understood. Obviously this is important.

Let's go back over each type of clarification individually. The first type, as we said, is: *Asking for more information.* It may be that the message of the speaker has been indirect or incomplete. The speaker might have said something like this: "I'm really angry." In this case, rather obviously, much information has not been supplied. No sensations or thoughts have been reported. No motivations or decisions have been mentioned. As a listener, I don't know to whom or at what your anger is directed. Are you angry at me? At someone or something else? What stimulated your anger? As a listener who wants to understand you and your message, I simply need more information. The only way I can get this information is to ask you, and so I do.

The way I ask is a very delicate and sensitive part of the process. I should seek further clarification only in "I statements" and yet still keep the focus on you. And so I will tell you why I am asking, but I will direct my remarks to an understanding of you rather than focus on my own confusion. For example, "I'm confused and I want to understand you more clearly." From such a beginning you will know what is stimulating my question, namely, my confusion. You will also know why I am seeking and what I am going to do with the added information, that is, understand you more clearly. If my problem and intentions are not clear to you, then we will both be confused and in the dark about each other. And in the search to find some light we will probably stumble into false assumptions and misconceptions. And from there it is only a short distance to blaming and other self-defensive maneuvers.

The following are two sample dialogues that demonstrate this first type of clarifying process. I'm sure you will notice that one is done destructively and the other constructively.

Sally: I'm really angry!

Joe: Why? I figured you were in a snit about something.

Sally: Well thanks for nothing. What do you mean: Why? If you were me, you'd be angry too!

Joe: Oh yeah! Well, it may interest you to know that I'm starting to get a little angry myself now.

If my problem and intentions are not clear to you, then we will both be confused and in the dark about each other.

Sally: I'm really angry!

Joe: I really do want to know what's going on with you.
               I hear your anger, but I don't know what happened.
               Could you help me out with a few details?

Sally: Yes, I think I can. It all started this morning . . .

To clarify a message when it is incomplete I will need to do two things. I must decide what type of information is not coming across: sensations, thoughts, feelings, motivations, decisions, actions, or even the activating event. Then I must tell you why I need the added information, what I need, and what I intend to do with it. It's really very simple. Our main concern should be to keep everything clear.

The second type of request for information, *Checking out word meanings,* deals with the diverse meanings and usages of words. At several places in this book we have discussed the uniqueness of individuals. This uniqueness is reflected in the "inner consistency" of each person, as well as in the distinctive "language" and "process" used by each person. These differences provide a real richness and diversity in the human experience. They also, however, can be a source of confusion in the communication process. The confusion, of course, arises from the fact that every single word I use has a definite meaning for me that is probably a shade or two different from the meaning you would attach to that word.

It is a temptation to expect that everyone understands all our meanings and word usages. It is far more realistic to accept our differentness as a fact. If I begin with this assumption, I will always expect to do some word clarifying when I am listening to others. For example, I recently read an article discussing whether personalities change after a certain age. The author concluded: It all depends on how you define *personality* and what you mean by the word *change*. Here are a few other examples:

Mark: They say it won't take very long.

Ann: I'm having a little trouble following what you just said. I'm not sure who you mean by *they*.

Mark: Oh, the guys at work. Two of them just went through the same thing we're going through.

Carol: I'm so anxious about Wednesday.

Ted: I'm puzzled. When you say you're anxious, do you mean that you are worried or excited?

Sue: It will really be a challenge for me.

Joan: I'm not sure what you mean by that. Is a challenge for you something you look forward to or something that you would dread?

Just imagine in each sample dialogue how the communication could have gone if the listener had not clarified certain words. I'm sure that you have experienced, as I have, whole conversations that got completely off the track. The speaker went in one direction; the listener in another. Then one or the other realized that the source of confusion was a difference in word definition. Sometimes this discovery is made during the actual exchange. At other times, unfortunately, it is made only on the next day or even years later.

Recently I saw an anonymous quotation hung on the wall of a local store. It seemed to express the frustration or maybe the humor in an exchange when the message is not getting across clearly from speaker to listener.

I know that you
believe you understand
what you think I said,
but,
I am not sure you realize
that what you heard
is not what I meant.

The third and last type of clarification is: *Verifying my understanding of your experience.* This approach is valuable when the information is complete and the word meanings are mutually understood but the whole "feeling tone" has not come across clearly. I'm not sure what effect the things you are sharing are having on you. I must remember that my goal as a listener is not just to understand what you are saying, but also to understand you. I want to know what it is like to be you. How do you perceive yourself, other people, and life? How do you experience certain events? To know these things I need to understand clearly all that you are trying to express. I want to be sure that the message you are sending is the message that I am receiving (message sent = message received). I want to make certain that I really understand all the dimensions of your sharing. Otherwise, we might be passing like ships in the night.

In this third type of situation, the listener perceives that listener and speaker are not sharing fully the experience being communicated. A shared experience with each other just isn't happening. In this case both people need patiently to go back and forth, piece by piece, and try to "live" the total communication together. The process in theory would go something like this:

1. The speaker shares the first part of the exchange.

2. The listener reflects back what is heard and what is not heard, what is clear and not clear.

3. The speaker acknowledges the part that was correctly heard and repeats in a new way what was not heard or not clear.

4. The listener reflects back his or her new understanding resulting from the clarification.

5. And so on until both speaker and listener are confident that a full understanding has taken place.

For example:

Jerry: I'd like to talk to you about the way I've been feeling about my job. The whole thing has really gotten to me lately.

Peggy: Oh, I'm really sorry to hear that. Is there a problem? What happened?

Jerry: It's not the problem I want to talk about. I would just like to sort out how I feel.

Peggy: Oh, I think I understand. You'd rather talk about your feelings. Is that it?

Jerry: Yeah, I think that's where I'm at. I've really had it with my boss and I hate the work I'm doing. I'm so bored I feel like I'm embalmed. It's like being on a treadmill. I just have no enthusiasm.

Peggy: You really seem down. Do you think of yourself as depressed or is that too strong a word?

Jerry: I guess I hate to admit to that feeling but, yes, I really think I am depressed.

Peggy: Oh, I think I'm with you now. I'd like to hear more about it.

This exchange could continue until the speaker is confident that all of the message to be shared has been heard by the listener. I think that most speakers probably have a sense about this and know when they have been clearly heard. And it is important to assure the listener of that. This last approach to clarity is usually reserved for very important issues.

Some precautions should be added about the use of these clarification processes. We should, of course, never interrupt the speaker in midsentence just to clarify the meaning of a word. Obviously we should wait till the speaker has finished sharing. Or, if there is an abundance of material, we should wait for an appropriate break to interject our clarifying questions. Any of the three types can be overused. Overuse will probably seem abrasive and produce self-consciousness or even irritation in the speaker. And reactions like these will probably short-circuit the whole communication process.

We should never expect or anticipate perfect understanding. This is humanly impossible. And if we overuse these clarifying approaches in an effort to insure such perfect understanding, our speaker will either give up on us or classify us among "nitpickers to be avoided." Instead, while listening to another we may begin to feel a sense of puzzlement and confusion. We may experience the temptation to make a risky assumption. All of these inner reactions are probably signals to us that there is a need for clarification.

The practice of these listeners' clarification processes can help us as speakers, too. When we are sharing, it is important that we supply the details our listener will need, that we define our meanings where they might be vague, and that we try to supply a "feeling tone" for our message.

In seeking a clarification on any of these three levels, the most important thing is that our intentions be clear to the speaker. And our intentions should always be:

- interest in the speaker,
- gentleness and patience with the process,
- and a desire to understand fully the sharing of another.

Passing like ships in the night is a lonely and painful alternative.

15

In the role of listener we should offer only suggestions and never directions.

(Note: This guideline does not pertain to the parenting of young children. Young children obviously need directions and a loving discipline that reinforces parental directions. But as they grow older there must be a gradual launching of the child into independent adulthood. As adults we must assume personal responsibility for our behavior and our lives. Such responsibility must be given over gradually to the child so that he or she can grow into a responsible adult.)

We human beings grow and develop into maturity in many ways. However, personal growth comes largely through the

exercise of our two specifically human powers: the mind and the will. We must be allowed to have our own thoughts, and to make our own choices. Of course, this clearly implies that at times we will think erroneously and we will make some poor choices. "To err is human ..." In a very true sense, if we are to mature we need the right to be wrong. Trial and error is the story of our very human lives. That's how we grow up.

The one sure way not to grow up is to hitchhike on the mind and will of someone else. We will never mature if we let others think for us and make our choices. Consequently, telling another what to think by interpreting reality for him or her is to forestall that person's maturation process. Likewise, telling another what to do is to aid and abet immaturity and a childish dependency.

More concretely, let's suppose that you come to me and tell me about a third party who is constantly in need of help. After listening long enough to form my own opinionated reactions, I interject, "Can't you see that he is just using you?" Even if I should be right in my split-second psychoanalysis of your friend, I am still telling you how to think. I am interpreting people and events for you.

Or let us suppose that you are faced with a decision, and you come to me. You ask me, "What should I do?" Being asked, I tell you, "There's no question in my mind. You should do A-B-C. And please let me know how it goes. (Translate:

The one sure way not to grow up is to hitchhike on the mind and will of someone else.

Report back to me.)" Again, my advice may possibly be on target, but even if it is, I am still giving you a prefabricated decision. You won't have to put it together for yourself. You won't have to grow up.

In either case, we both know, don't we, what you will do the next time a problem arises in your life. You have been coming to me for a "fix"; and the more you do it, the more you will depend upon it. You will become progressively more helpless and reliant on me. This could be a real temptation for me. I will feel very needed. I will bask in the soft sunlight of your gratitude and may even think that I am being very virtuous. After a while you and I will get locked into the roles of "helper" and "helpee." If I do this with many others, I will soon cultivate a whole clientele of dependent and mealy-mouthed souls who regularly come to me in need. Such an arrangement will postpone the maturity of all involved.

My own tendency to do just this was brutally exposed to me during a week-long communication workshop. One evening during this workshop all sixty of us participants were seated along the walls of a large square room. We were told to move into the center of the room only if and when we wished to, and to "let the music move your body." The process was clearly distinguished from dancing ("no partners") and we were told to move only those parts of our bodies ("head or arms or legs") that responded to the music played. Soon we began hearing music from a stereo. About half way through the first song, no one had stood up and moved into the center of the room. So I decided I would break the ice. After a few pirouettes, I noticed that everyone had joined me in the center of the room and was moving. I felt pleased with myself.

The next day, in our smaller group of six, the most obviously "fragile" member of our group suddenly burst into tears. She admitted to the group that if we were disappointed in her participation, she joined us in that disappointment. Amid her copious tears and heaving sobs, she assured us that if she had a deep, dark secret, she would gladly rip it out of her heart and share it with us. But alas! the poor dear did not even have such a secret. I remember melting with compassion. Immediately I assured her, "You are doing the best you can. That is all anyone can expect of you."

But our "facilitator," who usually circled the group with blood in her eyes, did not agree. Just as we had secretly named her the "Dragon Lady," so she had given all of us nicknames. Our fragile member had been dubbed "Goo-goo Eyes." The Dragon Lady loudly assured us that we had all been "suckers" and that Goo-goo Eyes had been manipulating us by her pretended weakness. She further insisted that Goo-goo Eyes knew very well how to participate in the interaction of the group, but was "copping out." The Dragon Lady further speculated that this manipulative cop-out was well practiced. "I'll bet she has been doing this all her life. She's really good at it."

Instinctively and gallantly, I rose to the occasion: "Hey, don't you think you're being kind of hard on her?" I asked. The response was terse and a real closeout. "Oh shut up, Loudmouth! (My nickname, can you believe?) You're next." So I resorted to slinking down in my chair to try for eye contact with Goo-goo Eyes. When I made contact, my eyes said, "I'm on your side." She read my message and replied verbally, "You know, she's right. I have been doing this all my life. I found out that when I say 'I just can't,' others never ask me 'Why?' They just let me get away with it."

Then the D.L. turned on Loudmouth. She asked me about the previous night and the "Music Move Your Body" exercise. "How did it feel to be the first one out on the center stage?" Without flinching I told her and the group about my ice-breaking intentions and about being pleased that "it worked." Then the Dragon Lady really turned up the heat. "Did you ever, even for a moment, think that if you had not gotten up, someone more shy and inhibited than you could have won a very valuable victory for himself or herself? But you didn't let that person win the victory. No, you had to win it for everyone!"

"Touché!" I thought to myself. But the Dragon Lady didn't wait for an answer. In fact, she didn't even take a breath. "And when I was working over Goo-goo Eyes, wouldn't it have been wonderful if she had spoken up for herself? Oh, but no, you spoke up for her. Didn't you?" ("Touché twice!") Seeing that she was on a roll, the Dragon Lady continued: "I'll bet you even go so far as to interpret situations for others and tell them what to do. Don't you?" I could immediately think of a thousand times when I had done just that.

Then I sat back and absorbed a lecture about how stupid this was, how it would create dependency in others and stifle their personal growth. Expensive food for my ego, she suggested, and I agreed. I should have known this workshop would be a little difficult when I noticed that it lasted five days and that only stable people between twenty-one and fifty would be accepted. I did not, however, anticipate the extent of the difficulty. But the lesson has stayed with me. I went home at the end and immediately resigned my Messiahship.

So what do you say when someone comes and you can see the hitchhiking thumb asking for a free ride? I sometimes have to work at stifling my old urge to turn into a computer printer spitting out all kinds of interpretations and advice. I have personally been working on the technique of the well-placed question. It goes something like this: "Gee, I don't know what you should do. What do you think? In your judgment, what are the possibilities?" Sometimes a suggestion can be successfully floated into the conversation by way of a question. "Say, did you ever think of going back to school and getting a degree?" Or, "Do you think your attitude toward authority figures has been affected by your relationship with your father?"

There are, of course, times when people are simply seeking information. "How many credit hours do I need to graduate?" If I have the needed information, I will be most happy to share it with those asking. However, when they come to the point of putting all their information together and making a decision that will affect their lives, the responsibility is all theirs.

A reminder in my memory bank reinforces my determination not to think or decide for others. I once met a middle-aged woman who was quite unhappy with her life situation. When I asked her how it had all come about, she told me that as a young girl she was assured that this was the life for her. So she embraced that way of life only to find out rather early on that she didn't like it. But her father (not the source of the original advice) commanded her, "You made your bed. Now you must lie in it." So she did, and with devastating effects. It is particularly distressing for any of us, I would think, to be living out someone else's decision for us.

Very recently a young man came to me with a cassette recording of his singing voice. It was a marvelous voice. He was obviously a very talented young man. Then he told me that those who are qualified to make such judgments have assured him that with training he could become one of the all-time greats of opera. However, he had been majoring in a distinctly different field in college, and he had been promised a relatively lucrative job in business. Then came the hitchhiking effort, veiled in probing questions. "What do you think I should do?" "If you were me, what would you do?" "In which life do you think I would be happier?"

We profitably discussed all the issues, I think, but he still has no idea of everything I was thinking. I assured him that his values are not mine, that what would make me happy might not make him happy. But all the time I knew that if God had given me his voice and if qualified people assured me as he had been assured, I would immediately plunge into an operatic career. But I am old enough and wise enough to know that I cannot think for or choose for anyone but myself. I am an expert only about myself. I must assume the responsibility to do my own thinking and make my own choices. However, I cannot do this for anyone else.

Do I want to play at being The Great Guru with a clientele of dependent people who need a regular "fix"? Uh, thanks but no thanks!

16

As listeners we should avoid all blocks to communication.

All of us, at times, use blocks of one kind or another to prevent ourselves from really listening to another person. We throw up barriers between ourselves and others. Obviously, once these blocks are erected, others can't receive any support or understanding from us. At the same time we also prevent ourselves from receiving the valuable gift of another's sharing. These blocks sabotage any real communication. Consequently, everyone involved is denied the chance to share and to grow.

The reasons we do this are various. I may be too preoccupied with my own agenda. I fear that if I concentrate on you, I will lose track of me. Or perhaps I fear that if the river of your pain runs into my world, I will be deluged. Open and true listening can prove costly. To open myself to receive another is always risky. Another common, if unconscious, motive for erecting blocks is our fear of intimacy. Although our hearts yearn for it, we also fear the possible consequences of human closeness. If I let someone get close to me, the other person may get a glimpse of the real me. It might blow my cover. I'm not sure that I'm ready for that.

At other times I don't really want to listen because I'm too impatient. I want to see problems get solved. I don't want to listen to an organ recital of feelings. That never seems to solve problems. Or it may be that I block the listening process because "I want to be stimulated or entertained and I find you boring." Then there's the familiar excuse: "I can't listen to you. I've got too many other more important things on my mind right now." I'm sure you can think of other motives for "blocking" communication. Some of our reasons are conscious; others may well be subconscious. But I feel sure that we all block out real listening on various occasions and for various reasons.

In order to eliminate these blocks it helps me to recall that every human being is a gift to be given. Communication is an act of gift giving. Picture it this way if you will. When I erect a block to the sharing process, I am refusing a gift graciously offered by another. It is as if someone is handing me a beautifully wrapped present. When I see it coming, I thrust my arms out stiffly in front of me to block the gift. Then I turn and walk away. It's a heavy truth to face, but this is what we do when we block another's communication. We equivalently say, "Don't bother me with your gift. I really don't want it." Obviously we should be saying, "Thank you for trusting me enough to share yourself with me."

We would like to make a partial list here of the most common blocks. A brief explanation of each is included along with a description of the usual result of each block. Some may seem foreign to you. Others you will recognize right away. Most have probably been used on us as well as by us. Our hope is that this review will make us all more aware of the times we may be throwing up these blocks. In this way we will learn more about our limitations as listeners. We will also be able gradually to eradicate our bad habits and become better listeners. Obviously, if we're unaware of a habit, we can't change it. So awareness must come first. If we are committed to communication, we certainly want to develop into listeners who do not block the process of communication. Awareness of our strengths and weaknesses will help.

The following is a partial listing of some common communication blocks.

ADVISING: "What you ought to do is . . ."

When we use this block of "advising," we probably think of listening as merely getting the facts about a problem. Once we have the facts, then we can solve the problem. We think people tell us things because they know we are inexhaustible mines of good advice. Advisers can't be bothered, of course, with feelings. "Just the facts, Ma'am." If this block to real

When I erect a block to the sharing process,
I am refusing a gift graciously offered by another.

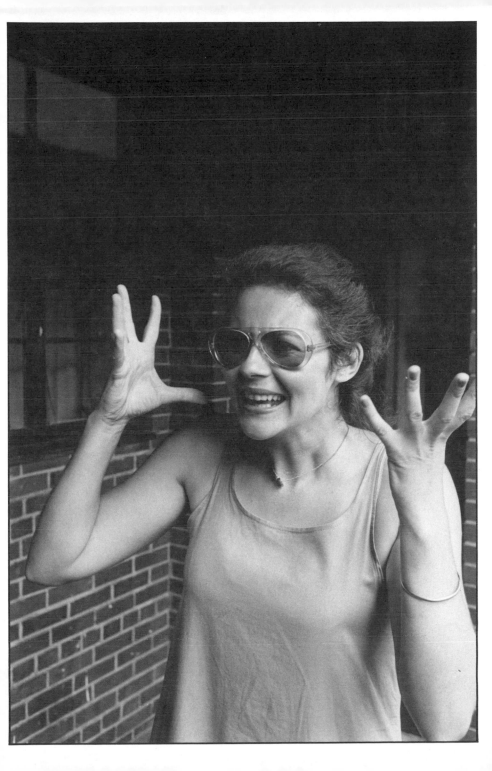

listening is consistently used, two possible results are most likely. Some more independent people will just stop sharing with a person whose consistent response is advice. Instead they will seek out another who will hear their feelings and respond empathically. Others who continue to share with the "adviser" will become more and more dependent and immature as the relationship progresses. Eventually they will forfeit all personal responsibility for thinking and deciding.

COMPETING: "I'm sure I look better than . . ."

If I'm competing while I'm listening, then I am assessing others in comparison to myself. I'm estimating their competence or mental health or kindness. Is it more or less than mine? Actually, I try to assess only those qualities about which I would come off looking better. While all this mental measuring is going on, I have very little time really to hear the other person. Does the other person feel heard? I may have become clever enough to fake some facial reactions and verbal responses. However, over time the speaker will catch on to me. So I can do my comparing only with acquaintances. People who have known me for a longer time have learned that I'm not a good listener. I don't really want to know them.

COMPUTING: "They say that studies have shown . . ."

If I am a computer type, I give only superresponsible, thoroughly accredited feedback. I always stay calm and provide very clear analyses of all my communications. I give liberal explanations with or without being asked. The person who is sharing with me may come to look upon me as a therapist. However, unlike therapists, I never deal with feelings. I rarely even hear them. In a dark room I have often been mistaken for a computer. This type of computing response blocks true communication by creating two problems. One is that you never get to know me. The other is that we will never be equals in our relationship. The growth that could occur from an honest sharing is stifled. People who spend a long time in my presence tend to feel very lonely.

DISTRACTING: "Say, this is a great place . . ."

When I use the distracting block of communication, I let you talk only for so long. As soon as I feel uncomfortable I switch the focus of the conversation. This unexpected shift will puzzle and distract you. Suddenly we are talking about something radically different. If I repeat this switching often enough, you will soon feel confused, angry, or possibly a little helpless. You may also get the impression that our conversation is really five conversations. You most likely will feel a bit rattled and rejected.

DREAMING: "What? . . . Oh sure . . . I understand."

Dreamers usually think of themselves as having good intentions. It is just that they often leave the hub of conversation and wander out onto one of the spokes of the wheel. The first thing mentioned connects with something else in the dreamer's mind. Then the free-association carousel begins to turn. One topic whisks the dreamer briskly to the next. If I am a dreamer, I'm having a wonderful time in my head. Sorry, though, it's a private party. Suddenly I tune in to you again and realize I've completely wandered away from and then rejoined the conversation. I hope you didn't notice. If you were talking just to hear your own voice, you may not have noticed that I was on a mental vacation. If, however, you were really counting on my understanding, you probably felt a little hurt that I was fading in and out on you. Subconsciously, I suppose I was looking for distractions. The personal involvement of a real conversation leaves me a little uneasy.

FILTERING: "Another good day at work, eh?"

When I use this block, I have to filter what I hear you say because I want to deal only with certain parts of you and your life. Before our conversation begins I have already decided what I will listen to and what I will tune out. If you start out on one of your personal weather reports, I become deaf. If we get to a subject that somehow threatens me, I pull out my hearing aid. Especially if you move into talking about intimacy or commitment, you may not know it but no one is listening. That blank look on my face reflects my thoughts perfectly. If you are a compulsive underdog in relationships and conversations, you'll probably accent even my crumbs of attention. Of course, this will reinforce your low opinion of yourself. If, however, you have a strong and positive sense of self, you won't settle for this shabby treatment. Either I will have to change or you will start looking for someone who really listens.

GUNNYSACKING: "Yes, but you . . ."

I have this huge gunnysack that I carry over my shoulder. I keep it with me at all times. For a long time I have been collecting grievances in it. All during our relationship I have made careful files of all my negative thoughts and feelings. Often I have made notes about the details that go with them too—date, time, day, place, and event. The compilation of this material has been my chief listening activity. When my nerves get frazzled or you have slighted me somehow, the gunnysack feels very full and heavy. My "poor me" attitude is in full bloom. And then I let go. I dump all my carefully collected garbage all over you. When this happens, you do whatever you can to put some distance between us. You may get angry, start an argument, pout, or just walk away in disgust. It really doesn't matter. I will continue filing and storing my hurts. And you'll hear about this one, too: you didn't accept my sharing. And so the cycle repeats itself. It might even be classified as comedy except that it always results in our growing apart.

IDENTIFYING: "Yes, that's like the time when I . . ."

With this block in place I politely excuse myself from careful listening. Maybe I can get away with no real listening at all. I pay attention to your words only until I find within them a jumping-off place for my own stories. It seems that my only real listening effort is temporary. I'd much rather be talking about me. So at my first opportunity I shift the focus to myself. I become the center of every conversation. Gradually you will realize your role is to be the listener. You won't get a chance to be the speaker. If you continue to relate to me, it will probably be out of pity. If you want "equal time," you will move on to someone who listens. In any case this block precludes a relationship of equality.

IGNORING: " . . ."

Even when I am "ignoring," I listen. You can never fault me for not listening. I just never deal with anything you say. I just let it hang in the air. Or, I let it go in one ear and out the other. You will never really know if I've heard you or not. Sometimes you will want to say, "Knock, knock, anyone home? I guess not." You won't know if I'm happy or hurting, interested or bored, in agreement or disagreement. I will give away no clues at all about my inner reactions to what you say. My nonresponse gives the suggestion that you and your sharing are totally irrelevant. Only a person with a desperately poor self-image will bother to talk to me. People looking for an honest exchange will feel frustrated by my blank face and silent voice. Certainly no one will ever feel understood by me. Likewise, no one ever gets to know me. I forever keep my own secrets. I live in a world that has a population of one.

NAME CALLING (labeling): "Oh c'mon, you're really paranoid."

To be really proficient at labeling, first I have to prepare the way by some generalizing and judging. But I'm well practiced at this. No matter what you have to say I can reduce you to a category. You see, I've already sorted humanity into certain types. It's very helpful. It makes people transparent, and it really simplifies relationships. As soon as you say enough for me to categorize you, that's it. I'm all set. You see, I have a whole set of judgments that go with each category. I've got these judgments in readiness too. After learning a few facts I can tell you who you are. My added implication is this: If you will only change your label, life and its problems will smooth out for you.

This marvelous labeling ability relieves me from the responsibility of listening. I don't have to wonder, "What is it like to be you?" You see, I know your type. I don't have to walk a mile in your moccasins. Moccasins come in certain sizes and styles. I've seen your kind before and they don't wear well. Once I've told you who you are, my involvement with you ends. I don't have to struggle with understanding. No pain, no gain. I never grow up. There is one strange thing. People avoid me. Only the most dependent people ever bother with listening to me.

PLACATING: "Oh yes. That's true. Uh huh, you're right."

If placating is my listening block of choice, it's because I know what is most important in a relationship. It's being liked and having peace at any price. You see, I want to be liked. So I'm always nice and consistently pleasant. I'm supportive and encouraging to everyone. All good qualities, eh? I can't stand conflict. Negative emotions make me nervous. I get quite tense with even mild disagreement. I insist that I don't have negative thoughts or feelings. Actually, I don't allow myself to hear them, either in me or in anyone else. For me, listening means to focus superficially on the words and give my immediate agreement. I never really listen deeply to learn who you are. If you're someone who wants only validation and agreement, you'll love me. However, if you're looking for a person you can bump into, a person who will be real with you, I'm not for you. You won't find such a person in me.

REHEARSING MY RESPONSE: "As soon as he's finished talking, I'm just going to tell him . . ."

In "rehearsing," I look as though I'm listening but I'm not really tuned in to you. All sharing for me is actually a win-lose contest. I am *semper fidelis,* always prepared to defend my image or my point. In fact, I have a knack for turning communications into debates. Whenever you're talking, I'm preparing my "equal-time" rebuttal. Of course, my statement has to make yours sound trivial. I have to come out on top. Consequently, I spend all my "listening" time rehearsing for my moment in the spotlight. Whatever you're saying is only a point of departure for my comments. If you also block listening by rehearsing, you might just enjoy the competition I will provide. We'll probably talk often with each other. However, we will never communicate our real selves. Only those puppets who like to hear me pontificate will stay with me. If you don't enjoy the game my way, you will get out of the sport completely. You will go looking for a real listener.

SARCASM (to cut flesh): "Don't hurry, Honey. You just might lose your image as Miss Holly Come Lately."

Sarcasm prevents me from dealing with real emotions and enjoying true intimacy. Now, if you are uneasy with emotions and afraid of intimacy, sarcasm will provide an effective barrier. But you'll have to be on guard. So many people want to be real. It can be very unsettling. If you let your guard down, these people might get close to you. You just can't let that happen, right? Better to push others away. But be prepared: you will even have to push away the real you.

The most effective way I know to create distance between us is to hurt you. However, I don't really want to come off as a mean person. Deep down I want people to like me . . . from a safe distance. So I combine my sharp tongue and sharp mind. If you get too close to the real me, I will "zap" you with a sarcastic remark. You may even laugh and find me entertaining. But you will learn to be careful with me. Sarcasm always works! You may stay in my vicinity for the entertainment. But you'll often feel angry, hurt, or sad when you're with me. Sarcasm stings. There may be times when you will feel sorry that I can't be real or allow intimacy. If sarcasm is my main listening response to others, I will never allow anyone to get close enough to know me. Most likely I will never know myself either.

You can probably think of other blocking strategies. Any behavior that sets up a barrier between speaker and listener is a block. It will prevent me from hearing what you have to share. You will never feel heard. I will never know that it's like to be you. There will be little real sharing between us. Our relationship can be only superficial. To avoid this sadness we must examine our own listening. Which blocks do I use the most? With whom? When? Why? How can I exchange my habit of building barriers for a new habit of open listening?

Honest answers to these questions can make a great difference in our lives. Such answers could mean the difference between stagnation and growth. A block is a block is a block is a . . .

17

We should explicitly thank those who have shared themselves with us.

Under our second guideline, it was suggested that we learn to think of ourselves as gifts to be given and to think of others as gifts offered to us. Consequently, guideline number eight recommended that we explicitly thank those who have listened to us. Empathic listening is always a true gift. It assures us that someone wants to stand with us, to share our experience. It is painful to be alone and to feel estranged.

However, it feels even more risky and frightening to put our own most sensitive confidences in the hands of another. And so, when we are the recipients of another's sharing, it is very important to be explicitly grateful. We have just received an important and valuable gift: part of another human being and another human life. Consequently, we should practice the habit of thanking others for their self-disclosure and for their trust in us.

When the self-disclosure is an obvious risk (the confiding of a deep and dark secret), gratitude comes most easily. It is likewise pleasant and easy to acknowledge a self-disclosure that affirms us and our worth. It gets a bit more difficult when the sharer offers to take us into the valleys of his or her sadness or depression. It is also difficult to feel grateful when others share with us their problems, personal labyrinths that seem to have no exit. It is important, of course, not to take on these

problems of others and to make them our own. Nevertheless, it is always difficult to have a box seat in the arena where someone is fighting for his or her life.

The situation in which it is most difficult to be openly grateful, I would think, is one created by a self-disclosure that is indirectly or directly critical of us. Most of us are well practiced in being defensive. It is almost as instinctive as blinking our eyes when something brushes by our faces. If we feel attacked, something in us seems to rise to our own defense. I suppose that this instinct is traceable to our proverbial inferiority complexes. Criticism is only another blow on an already sore place. In general, the more we suffer from a sense of inferiority, the more defensive we become. Only the self-confident seem to retain their composure under attack.

And yet most of us know how hard it is to express our negative reactions. When someone does bring up an issue that implies some failure on our part or some negative reaction to our persons, we can be sure that this person has probably had to work up extra courage to share these negative-type feelings. It is therefore especially important for us to be explicitly grateful for such a sharing.

There are many problems and pitfalls in the growth of a human relationship. Our handling of negative reactions is critical. It is extremely important to react gratefully when the sharing of another implies a failure on our part or some

It is difficult to feel grateful
when others share with us their problems,
personal labyrinths that seem to have no exit.

negative reaction to our persons. If others can't share with us their negative reactions, but have to keep them bottled up inside themselves, this repression will eventually sour their feelings for us. In the end it will challenge the very commitment of their love. And if we plant our feet or set our jaws every time others try to open up such thoughts or feelings, they will soon want to give up on communication with us.

Of course, negative *judgments* are always "out of order" in a relationship. For example, I will not say of you or allow you to say of me, "You are a very proud and selfish person. You never think of others. And you really neglect me!" That would not be speaking only *your* truth. It would be quite different if you were to say, "There are times when I feel neglected. I do not feel your concern for me." For such honesty and openness I must be grateful. If I were to react defensively rather than gratefully to this latter statement, you would find it even harder to share honestly and openly with me in the future. You would be strongly tempted to keep your negative feelings to yourself, and this would be the beginning of the end of our relationship. It always is.

I remember a young woman coming to see me at a time when I ordinarily am not available. I thought of myself as "walking an undemanded mile" for her. As I was listening to her very open and honest sharing, I occasionally registered signs of understanding how the pieces fit together. Little "Ohs" and "Ahs!" After an hour or so she left with an exchange of very pleasant remarks. Some minutes later, she returned to say, "I just wanted to add that I didn't feel listened to tonight. My reaction was that you listened only long enough to categorize me. I felt angry at the thought of having my communication sorted and filed under definite headings. I don't know if you really weren't listening or if you really were categorizing me, but anyway that was my interpretation and reaction."

What do you think? Was that good communication? Should she have left this unsaid? My own response was, "Hey, thank you for having the courage to tell me that. It must have been difficult, but you said it well. I don't really know if I was listening to you in the right way. My first reaction is that I was not simply categorizing you. However, I will certainly think about it. But for now I can only be grateful for your honesty and your trust in me." I think that if she had not been able to say these things or if I had reacted in a defensive, hurt, or angry way, the relationship might have been threatened. The lines of communication between us might have fallen.

If I do think of you as a gift to be given and if I do think of your sharing with me as the giving of that gift, I will certainly want to thank you. In addition to the contents of your sharing, you also give me your trust. You trust me with an honest and open sharing of yourself. Obviously you are taking the risk of personal vulnerability. You are aware of the possibility that I could reject you or ridicule your sharing. I could react badly, looking hurt or angry or expressing disappointment in you. I might even refuse to listen to your sharing. Yet in sharing yourself you hold out your offering in uncertain, trembling hands. Thank you, thank you, thank you.

> *"Ingratitude is sharper than a serpent's tooth."*
> *King Lear,* Act 1, Scene 4

PART FOUR

General Practices That Promote Good Interpersonal Communication

18

Good communication requires that the communicators spend special or quality time together.

Have you ever tried to tell something important to another person in a train station when you had very little time? Besides the time crunch the train was pulling out of the station, and some of the passengers were excusing themselves to get by you. Still others were pushing and shoving, and some were even close enough to overhear what you wanted to say. Do you remember a circumstance like this and do you recall how frustrated you felt? If so, then you know what "special" and "quality" time means and why it is required for good communication.

Quality time implies that there is no time crunch and there is no crush of a crowd around you. In quality time we can search confidently for just the right words that express what we are thinking and feeling. We have the leisure to look for and get in contact with the things that lie buried deep within us. Most of us find self-disclosure difficult, even when we don't have to worry about a time deadline and other distractions.

It is scary to tell another person the things we have kept hidden in the darkness for a long time. And so it helps to find a time and place where there is no rush and there are no distractions. It is easier to get in touch with our hidden secrets and to explore our inner spaces when we have quality time. We are better at communication when taking a long walk or a leisurely drive in the country. It is easier to locate the hidden pieces of our human puzzle while sitting together at the close of the day. By this time the dust of daily struggle has settled and the duties of the day have been discharged.

We also need an unhurried and undistracted listener, one who can provide us with "presence" and "availability." It is always much easier to share ourselves when we know someone cares enough to listen. In a very real sense the quality of the time regulates the quality of listening. And the quality of listening directly affects the quality of sharing.

Almost all of us know that we usually get those things done which we really want to do. We always seem to find time for the things we enjoy. However, we also usually find excuses to put off the things for which we feel an aversion. A friend of mine who is involved in education openly admitted to me

Quality time implies that there is no time crunch and there is no crush of a crowd around you. In quality time we can search confidently for just the right words that express what we are thinking and feeling.

that the one difficult part of his job is the "annual financial report." We laughed together as he told me about his schemes of avoidance. First he gets as far as his typewriter. Then he realizes that his calculator really should have new batteries. So he goes to the store to buy new batteries, and dawdles there, looking for excuses to delay getting back to the dreaded financial report. Back at the typewriter, he types one line and notices that the typewriter ribbon is worn. However, he looks at his watch and decides that it is too late to go back to the store. And so the financial report gets put off for one more day. Most of us can recognize something of ourselves in this example.

One solution is to chart a daily schedule for the following day. We have to schedule into our day the quality time for communication. We have to give it a high priority and reserve a special time when good communication can take place. Otherwise we will go looking for calculator batteries and typewriter ribbons. And in the end we will have lost something far more valuable than anything else. Again it is the haunting question: Do we really want to communicate?

The participants in Marriage Encounter have a unique way to guarantee this type of quality time for sharing. They take ten unhurried minutes out of their day to write each other a short note of sharing. Sometimes they agree in advance on the topic, like "How do I feel when you touch me?" Or "What is the quality in you that I admire most?" Then at day's end, during quality time, they exchange notes. These notes become a good springboard for personal sharing.

A man and woman who have been united for many years in what I consider a healthy marriage relationship once shared with me an important factor in the success of their life together. On their wedding day they mutually acknowledged the importance of quality time. So they added to their vows a solemn promise to each other that unless it was absolutely impossible, they would spend some time alone together each day. In further description of this quality, reserved time, they told me, "We have never used this time to discuss practical details such as grocery shopping. We confine our discussions to ourselves and our relationship." I remember that they also said, "Sometimes life got pretty stormy. But our reserved time together was always the eye of the storm, our hidden place of peace and calm."

I have personally experienced the importance of this quality time. In the last years of my mother's life, she was pretty much confined to her bed. During my weekly visits I would sit by her bed and we would chat about various things. There was no place to go and nothing to distract us. Only ourselves. Usually I would start out by sharing some part of myself that sometimes puzzled even me: my mood swings, my fear of dying, and so forth. She was a good listener and allowed me the time to draw out of myself many personal thoughts and feelings that I had not previously recognized. Everything human is contagious, so Mother would then tell me about herself, about her peaceful acceptance of dying but her fear of pain.

Mother could locate in herself no fear of dying. ". . . ever since you kids were raised," she said. She did share with me a long-standing, almost morbid fear of pain. She confided, "I have asked God, when he comes for me, to kiss me softly while I am sleeping. I dread the thought of a painful, gasping-for-breath kind of dying." Twenty-four hours before she actually did die, Mother lapsed into a coma. The doctor told us that she would not come out of her coma, but would die in her sleep. I thought to myself, "God is going to kiss you softly while you are sleeping. I guess he could refuse you nothing." When death finally came, I cried the kind of tears we cry at the recognition of something beautiful: my mother and our relationship. However, I am aware that much of this valuable sharing came about while sitting in her quiet room, by her bedside, during our "quality" times together.

A confirmation of this need for quality time took place in my exposure to what is called "reevaluation counseling." A teacher of this method, who is also my friend, explained it to me. She told me that any relatively compatible couple can get together regularly and set equal time allotments for sharing. It is important that both take the same amount of time so that one doesn't become the therapist and the other the client. It is also important to do this at a conducive time and in a conducive place.

Then, my friend told me, each of the two goes back to a time and an experience in the past when he or she could not or did not express the deep emotions of that moment. For example, they might share a time when they were humiliated as small children by a tyrannical teacher, but could not express their fear or outrage. An important assumption of this reevaluation counseling is that our psychological scars are largely due to unexpressed emotions or feelings.

But the time of healing is at hand if we can recreate the scene in our mutual sharing, and relive the experience. Only this time we will reevaluate the experience from a more adult perspective and we will give full expression to the emotions that had to be stifled at the time of the original experience. My friend explained that it is important not to interrupt or to attempt to comfort each other. This would tend to stifle the expression of emotions and so minimize the cleansing and the healing of the old wounds.

She then invited me to try this method with her. I agreed and we decided that each of us would take one half hour. First my friend told me about some almost unbelievable experiences of her childhood life. In the shared retelling and reliving of the incidents, she shed the tears she could not cry as a child. She trembled and whimpered as these old and buried experiences were being relived and exposed to the light of sharing. I must admit that I wondered how my friend could have gone through all the described experiences and have turned out so well adjusted. I now presume that the sharing of reevaluation counseling has had much to do with it.

When her half hour had passed, I felt empty and somehow superficial. I had nothing to share that was comparably traumatic. I felt as though I had no tears to cry, no trembling to release. So I started out to share my stereotypical stories. However, in the presence of a good listener, I soon found layers and layers of previously unexpressed emotions. I might never have found them if I hadn't known that I was expected to fill out the half hour. I remember at the end feeling a great sense of relief. It was certainly a very valuable hour of my life. But it could not have happened, I think, if we had not set aside that hour for uninterrupted sharing. There were no deadlines to meet, no decisions to make, no tasks to be completed. It can happen only in quality time, set aside for the important exchange of personal sharing. It can hardly happen in a train station when the crowds are pushing and the train is pulling out.

The desire and determination to set aside such special time will be proportioned to our desire for communication. And so some interior searching is in order here. If this idea is not appealing to me, it may well be that I really do not want to communicate. It may be that I fear true intimacy. It may be that I do not understand the need for deep communication in order to have a fulfilling relationship and a satisfying life. The answers are inside me, waiting to be discovered.

Special times may be the wisest investments we can make.

19

Touching is an important form of communication.

At times the slightest touch can say something, can express a warmth that words cannot convey. Everyone has no doubt heard of the effects that the lack of physical affection has on a baby. Newborns who experience no physical affection usually get sick and even die. It is also a fact that deprivation of touching can result in allergies, eczema, speech problems, and learning problems. Obviously, touching is one of our most powerful and primary means of communication. And what is called "skin hunger" is a recognized fact of human life. Sometimes children ask to have their backs scratched or their feet rubbed more for the reassurance of physical contact than for alleged reasons. Adults, too, often ask to have their shoulders or scalps massaged just to be reassured that someone cares. Affectionate touching offers this reassurance.

In their book *The Stress-proof Child*, Saunders and Remsberg insist that it is impossible to overemphasize the important connection between touching and a sense of security. The authors see the experience of being touched as an essential contribution to a person's security and self-esteem.

> *This is an old lesson that is being rediscovered by modern psychologists. Touching is how infants learn to feel good about themselves. It is a means by which parents can say to older children, "I really like you."*
>
> quoted in *Reader's Digest,* July 1985, p. 156

There are those of us who feel threatened by touch. Such persons regard touching as an invasion of personal space and privacy. They have obviously grown up in nondemonstrative families. Consequently, they tend to be put off by all this "touch-feely" stuff. "Let's not start that," they protest. There is also in our sex-drenched society a suspicion that touching usually has hidden sexual overtones. In a recent discussion of the current epidemic of the sexual abuse of small children, an important point has been strongly made. We must not overreact, thinking that all touching is harmful to children. Children need to sit on Grandpa's lap and be cuddled by Grandma. They need honest hugs and loving kisses from people who care about them.

Obviously, touching solely for our own sexual gratification without the personal dimension of caring is only a selfish demand for service. It is a signal without subtlety. It is also a misuse of touching. Self-centered touching is not really communication. It is much like a lie, which is a misuse of the faculty of speech. It is a lie to say "I love you" only as a form of manipulation to gain selfish gratification. The same thing would be true of the touching that is only a ploy. It is as much a misuse of touch as a brutal punch in the nose.

However, the physical has always been suspect. Literature of the past has assured us that the body is the ugly prison of the sweet soul. The three sources of human temptation have been depicted as "the world, *the flesh,* and the devil." And yet in our normal way of knowing, nothing can come into the soul without coming through the channels of the body and the antennas of the physical senses. Without our senses we could never have ideas, at least not in the normal way of human knowing. Body and soul constitute a unity and harmony, not a dichotomy. One without the other is incomplete.

Probably under all our real or imagined fears is the fear of true intimacy. The fear of intimacy is always with us. Somehow we sense that touching can be a strong bonding force. Bonding leads to and results from commitment. Commitment,

of course, implies obligation. And the obligation of commitment is scary to most of us. So we sense and fear the
consequences of affectionate touching. It has even been
suggested by reputable authors that real intimacy is so scary
that we use waving to others or clapping hands in applause
for them as nervous substitutes for actual touching. The same
has been said about playful wrestling and scuffling.

Those of us who grew up in demonstrative families know
that holding hands, hugging, and physical signs of affection
are important means of communicating. We know that
touching adds a whole new dimension to verbal communication. We are "bodily" human beings, a close composite of
body and soul which work together in close cooperation.
We should think of our senses as gifts of God and antennas
of learning. In fact, one of the laws of learning is that the
more senses involved in the learning process, the deeper the
lessons will penetrate and the longer they will be remembered. Please take a moment and recall the sensory images
of your own childhood: being carried up to bed and tucked
in, being kissed and consoled when you fell down, riding high
up on Daddy's shoulders, or holding on tightly to Mama's
hand in a crowded department store. Images of safety and
security.

When it comes to self-esteem and security, we need all the
assurances we can get. And so we need to hear kind words,
to see smiles and feel the tenderness of loving touches. When

Somehow touching bridges our feeling
of separateness and aloneness
more effectively than words.

these sense reassurances are withheld, we grow insecure and we do not feel comfortable about ourselves. One juvenile court judge has made this observation about touching. This judge had presided over the same juvenile court for more than twenty years. On the day of "sentencing," he related, the parents of the juvenile offenders would usually come to court. The judge remarked that in all his years on the bench he had never once seen a parent touch his or her child who was standing in judgment. He then admitted to wondering if that might not be why the young person was in court in the first place.

We do know about this need for touching and being touched in chimpanzees and monkeys, primates who are most like us in physical structure. When they are deprived of physical touching, they become neurotic, irritable, and unable to relate. This fact has been clearly demonstrated in repeated experiments.

Somehow touching bridges our feeling of separateness and aloneness more effectively than words. A hidden-camera movie was made recently in a college library. The young woman at the desk was told to treat the first ten people coming to the desk in a polite and efficient manner. However, she was told to be careful about *not* touching them. With the next ten, she was asked to exhibit the same polite, efficient manner but somehow to make a slight physical contact with them. As they turned in or took out books, she was to let her hand brush quickly against theirs.

Outside, an interviewer waited to ask the subjects of the experiment this question: "Was the girl at the desk friendly?" The first ten, who had not experienced any physical contact, admitted that she was efficient and polite. However, they said that they could not call her "friendly." The second ten, who were treated in the exact same manner with the addition of a slight touch, were quick to insist, "Yes, she was very friendly."

I have often thought that touch is to communication what music is to words. Singing "Happy Birthday" has a certain warmth and sense of celebration. Reciting "Happy Birthday" somehow just doesn't make it. Trying to communicate at an hygienically safe distance, without any physical contact, may in the end seem as sterile as a routinely recited "Happy Birthday."

Some frightened part of us wants to avoid the personal closeness of human intimacy. Touching has consequences, and we sense that human bonding is brought about by our touching and being touched. It is a very important form of communication. Something in us seems to know that very well.

So let's reach out and touch someone.

20

To become more effective communicators we must "stretch" beyond our "comfort zones."

A couple of the terms in this guideline represent a highly personalized usage, and should be explained. The last shall be first, so let us start with "comfort zones." It has been said that all of us live in a comfort zone. Try to imagine a circle, big or small, that represents a comfort zone. Then put a dot inside the circle. The dot is you or I and the circle is our comfort zone. We can move around inside the circle and feel comfortable there, but if we move out of the circle, we suffer a panic attack. We are insecure outside that area and feel threatened.

Comfort zones encompass the way we dress and our personal appearance in general. They determine what we can and cannot do. They have a strong effect on the way we deal with people and so forth. A "neatnik" like Felix Unger in *The Odd Couple* would feel uncomfortable in slovenly dress, but roommate Oscar Madison's shoes would immediately become uncomfortable if he shined them. In describing the circumference of our comfort zones, some of us say, for example, "Oh, I just can't give a speech in public," or "The thought of walking into a roomful of strangers terrifies me," or "Maybe someone else can do it, but that's just not me." Sometime make a list of things you just "cannot do." It will give you some idea of the size of your comfort zone. I was surprised by some of those on my list.

The problem is that we huddle carefully inside that comfort zone; and if it is small, then we are imprisoned in a small world. However, most of us would rather stay in our prisons than pay the price of discomfort for venturing out. We allow ourselves to be painted into a small corner of life. We never find out the limits of our abilities because we never explore them. We don't enjoy our full capacities because we never really test them. It has been said that the average person uses only 10 percent of his or her abilities. The other 90 percent gets buried in graves of fear. We fear failure. We fear making a fool out of ourselves. We fear the ridicule of others. We fear criticism. So we cave in and settle down in our comfort corner, and every day begins to look pretty much like yesterday and tomorrow. We wear the same clothes, say the same things, meet the same people, go through the same routines because that is where we are comfortable.

At first it sounds a bit shocking to say, "We must try to overcome all our inhibitions." Sometimes inhibitions are construed as fortunate fences that keep us bound in on the "straight and narrow" paths of virtue. But there is no virtue in inhibition, simply because there is no freedom. For example, I might say something like: "Oh, I just could never tell a lie. I'm sure my cheeks would flush and my nose would grow." I am inhibited. I am held back from lying by the fear that I would not be a successful liar. If this is the case, there is no virtue in my telling the truth. I couldn't do otherwise. Virtue presumes and requires freedom. "I could lie to you, but I choose not to. I want to be a truthful person." This would be an expression of true virtue.

Of course, we don't want to overcome our inhibition to lie by lying. That would really be not letting the left hand know what the right hand is doing. But there are other inhibitions that keep us from freedom and virtue, and these should be directly assaulted by what we call "stretching." For example, a person might say, "I just can't tell those I love that I do love them. So I try to do things for them, to give them gifts. But the words 'I love you' just stick in my throat." The course and the challenge to stretch are clear. "DO IT AND DO IT NOW!" In the consistent practice of this attack on such crippling inhibitions, one eventually becomes a much freer person. And soon he or she will be doing things because "I want to and not because I just couldn't do otherwise." This is a fully human and fully alive person. This is a truly liberated and virtuous person.

"To stretch," as we use the term here, means "to step outside our comfort zones." It means to dream the impossible dream, to reach for the previously unreached, to try the untried, to risk the possibility of failure, to dare to go into places where we have never been. Obviously, one has to

understand clearly the meaning and the advantages of stretching. This is especially true in the beginning, because stretching requires a strong act of the mind and will. I have often imagined our emotions as children surrounding their parents, Mother Mind and Father Will. Often children try to walk tightrope on high fences, to peek over cliffs, and to pet grizzly bears. They kick and cry and squeal when they are not allowed to start dangerous bonfires or throw sharp knives. Mother Mind and Father Will have to be strong and determined. Some parents have insisted that insanity is, in fact, inherited: You get it from your children.

When a person first attempts this challenge of stretching, of stepping out of old comfort zones and into new areas, the children (the emotions) will certainly act up. They will start kicking and screeching, crying and protesting. The imagination (an interior sense) will paint ugly pictures of embarrassment and failure. It will make frightening sounds. "The world will end with a 'big bang!' At least there will be a big explosion. Someone, probably me, will definitely faint. Murphy's Law ('What can go wrong will go wrong!') will once more prevail."

But if Mother Mind and Father Will are strong enough, they will prevail. And believe it or not, the world won't go up in smoke. There will be no explosion. No one will faint or die. And old Murphy won't even show up. But that's only some of the things that won't happen. What will result from our stretching is that the world will be widened for us, and our lives will become fuller and more satisfying. Talents will be

"To stretch," as we use the term here,
means "to step outside our comfort zones."
Stretching requires a strong act of mind and will.

revealed that we didn't even know we had. Do you remember the first time you swam without someone holding you afloat or the first time you hit a home run? "I can do it!" you announced to yourself and to the world. You didn't drown and you didn't strike out. You did it! A new self-confidence and a new world were created for you in that moment. It always happens when we stretch.

What does all this have to do with communication? Obviously there are many risks and challenges in this area. They invite us to stretch, to step out of the old and into the new. All progress in human growth always involves some stretching. Here's a partial list of communication challenges that may be inviting you and me to stretch. Some of these may apply to you or me; others may not. Please look them over.

- To think of myself as a gift to be given; to regard others as gifts given to me.

- To tell someone face-to-face: "I love you."

- To take full responsibility for my own reactions; to express them by making "I statements" and not "You statements."

- To admit I was wrong, and to apologize; to ask for forgiveness.

- To own and to share all my feelings, negative and positive.

- To share my vulnerability: to tell others of my fears and foibles, to stop lying about my loneliness, to admit my insecurity and to say "ouch" when I am hurt, to let tears flow through my protective mask.

- To work at being real by recognizing and rejecting my "role," by refusing to let my role playing edit the communication of the real me.

- To check out with utter honesty my motives as far as I am able; to make sure my communication is an act of love, not a ventilation or a manipulation.

- To thank others for their listening and/or sharing.

- To really listen: with head, heart, and imagination.

- To wonder: What is it like to be you?

- To check out assumptions rather than attributing X-ray accuracy to my mind reading.

- To refuse to give advice; to insist that others, who ask me what to do, make their own decisions.

- To avoid sarcasm, blaming, pouting, having temper tantrums in order to punish and manipulate others.

- To make out a schedule that includes "quality time" with those to whom I am closely committed.

- To touch and allow myself to be touched as an act of caring and communication.

- To be so committed to communication that I will not allow a crisis to shake my resolve.

It is important to repeat that stretching is appropriate only when the inhibition prevents us from saying, doing, or being what is *right and reasonable*. Stretching does not ask us purposefully to make ourselves look foolish or to do counterproductive deeds just for the sake of stretching. Being a "nut" is not the same as being a growing person.

I keep thinking about all the great men and women in our human history. Imagine Joan of Arc whimpering, "But I can't ride a horse, let alone lead an army!" What if Christopher Columbus had said, "I can't be right and all those people wrong. What if I fail and get lost on the high seas? What will other people say about me then?" Suppose that Thomas

Jefferson had caved in to his fears: "Write a Declaration of Independence for a new country? You're kidding. I've never written a Declaration before."

Now you might react by saying, "Yes, but they were great and famous people. I'm neither great nor famous." To which I am tempted to reply, "Right. But neither were they before they stretched!"

In your life and mine there are a thousand challenges of communication inviting us to step out of our present confinement. My own kindergarten teacher is alive and well and living in Chicago. She tells me that I (John) was the "shyest and skinniest" kid she had ever taught in some thirty years in the classroom. Of course, she saw only the outside of me. I was inside that little kid, suffering, sneaking glances, worried about what others were thinking, afraid to look bad, playing it safe, and trying to pretend I was something I really wasn't.

Fortunately, I have been influenced by several people like that teacher. They challenged me lovingly. I remember that Walter Cronkite was once asked, "Outside your family, who was the most influential person in your life?" The famous newscaster reflected for a moment and then said, "I think it was my fourth grade teacher." For myself, I am most grateful to my kindergarten teacher, Catherine Ford Barr. And I am also grateful to all those like her who told me that I could do it, and then challenged me to try.

Now that "shyest and skinniest" kid often addresses large audiences with a peaceful self-confidence. Sometimes his "child" blinks and wonders about all this, but the milestones of stretching remind him of the "less traveled road" that made all the difference. The first halting speeches at student assemblies, the cold hands and dry mouth of the elocution contests, nervously getting ready for the debate tourneys, and eventually winning the senior high school oratorical contest.

When others attempt to rationalize their inhibitions and to tell me that "they just can't," that "stretching is too much" for them, the shyest and skinniest kid in kindergarten wants to confront them. He wants to challenge them lovingly to stretch as he was challenged to stretch. Now that shy little kid has more mileage on his mouth than an antique automobile. Now when he stands up before large audiences, he is a racehorse at the gate, ready and eager to go.

But this pertains only to public speaking. In the area of person-to-person communication I still suffer from the cramps of my comfort zone. So every day I try to do at least one little stretching exercise. I know that this is the price of my freedom and my realness as a person. So I try to admit it when I don't know, I apologize when I blunder, I own my own feelings, I tell others how good and gifted they are, I openly acknowledge my fears and hurts, and I work at wondering what goes on in those I meet. Gradually I am improving as a communicator. I am not a great success yet, but I know the way. There are no rules for success that work unless we do. So every day we have to stretch a little, and every day our ease with and facility for communication will grow.

It does work. Take it from the shyest and skinniest kid in kindergarten.

21

We must be ready to apologize when an apology is appropriate and helpful.

Admitting our failures and asking to be forgiven is an almost magical formula to remove many of the obstacles to good communication. A sincere apology instantly dislodges all the defensive techniques which are the death of dialogue. Also an apology shares, as nothing else can, our personal vulnerability. Yet most of us find it very difficult to apologize. Some fear lurks deep within most of us that makes an honest admission of our mistakes difficult.

It goes without saying that this fear will be different in different people. We are all haunted by different demons. One person might be disturbed by an anticipated "loss of face." Another might feel threatened by the fear that the other person will misuse the apology. "If I apologize to you, you might remind me of my admission during some heated argument in the future. You might use my apology with a vengeance. I don't want my apology to become a scourge in your hand. I don't want to be reminded of my mistakes or punished for my honesty." In most of us, I feel sure, this inability to apologize is directly related to our feelings of inferiority. Alfred Adler, you will remember, theorized that we spend most of our energies and lives trying to prove that we are all right.

Most of us find it very difficult to apologize. Some fear lurks deep within most of us that makes an honest admission of our mistakes difficult.

All I know is that some vague fear seems to inhibit my own ability to say, "I was wrong. I'm sorry." When I try to remember the last several times I sincerely apologized, I have to go a long way back. My undercover thinking is that the other person involved has never apologized to me. Then I mentally review all the times when this would certainly have been appropriate. If I haven't received the apologies due to me, why should I offer any? It's the old deception of being a reactor instead of an actor. It's the immaturity of letting another person's behavior determine my own. Somehow I let someone else's failure to apologize decide how I am going to act.

Certainly part of our difficulty with apologizing is the problem we have with interior honesty. To get to the moment and act of apologizing, I must first be very honest with myself about my failures and limitations. Without a relentless effort at interior honesty, I can only deceive myself and deceive you. We have already discussed the ego-defense mechanism of rationalization. When rationalizing, we cannot look at the truth objectively. We are too busy working out a construct of self-justification. "You had it coming. You did the same thing to me three weeks ago. I'm only giving you a taste of your own medicine." Most of us get lost in the endless circles of rationalization. We twist the truth, launder our language, and even falsify the facts. And all this labor is designed simply to justify ourselves and to whitewash our mistakes. And once the rationalization is completed, there is no more need for an honest admission of failure or an apology.

To avoid the dishonesty of the rationalization process, I must ask myself: Do I accept the real me, the flawed and imperfect me, the one who limps, the broken me? Do I really accept myself as a mistake maker? Have I learned how to laugh at myself and my "klutziness"? I have to think about this very seriously. Unless and until I do so accept myself, I cannot be truly honest or real. And if I am not real, my life will become one prolonged charade. As the song lyrics say:

When we played our charade
We were like children posing,
Playing a game,
Acting a name,
Guessing the part we played.

I would like to suggest another thought about apologies and forgiveness for your consideration: I am subjectively certain that whenever there is trouble in a relationship, a failure to apologize and a lack of forgiveness are involved. I am likewise sure that whenever the lines of effective communication have fallen, the same two failures—the failure to apologize and the failure to forgive—will only prolong the estrangement.

There is a family ritual, used by native Hawaiians, called *ho'oponopono.* The word itself means "setting right" or "making right." The ritual was designed by the ancient Hawaiians to restore and maintain good relationships among the members of a family. The specific family conference of this ritual involved prayer, discussion, confession, repentance, mutual restitution, and forgiveness. Once a year or whenever a serious problem arose, the members of a family were invited to participate in the rite of *ho'oponopono.* If an individual wanted to remain a member of the family, he or she came to the ritual. No excuses were considered valid.

The rite began with prayer (*pule*) to God (or the gods). The members of the family prayed for the necessary help to be honest in self-scrutiny. The whole rite necessarily supposes a quality of absolute truthfulness and sincerity. The Hawaiians called this *'oia'i'o:* the very "spirit of truth." Then there was an honest confession or admission by each person of wrongdoing, grievances, grudges, and resentments. If restitution was in order, this was to be done immediately or plans were made to have it done in the very near future. Forgiveness of all was sincerely requested in the form of an apology and granted in an explicit act of forgiveness. This forgiveness was seen as a "release" from guilts, grudges, and tensions. The Hawaiians who still practice this ritual today see the whole rite as one of: the asking for forgiveness, the granting of forgiveness, and the release of all involved. And once this is done, the matter is finished and forgotten. It is never to be acted upon or brought up again. The Hawaiians have always known that the help of God would be needed for this, and so the ritual is ended with a prayer that love and peace will once more characterize the family relationships.

So many of the features of this ancient Hawaiian ritual seem to correspond to our modern experience. We need all the help we can get to be honest with ourselves. The spirit of truthfulness must be present in all sincere apologies. Then we must strive to make an honest admission of our failures to others who have been hurt or offended by our mistakes. "I was wrong. I am sorry. Please forgive me." I think it is very rare that forgiveness is ever withheld when one sincerely admits a mistake and asks for forgiveness. When sought and granted, this forgiveness then becomes a source of release. The record book has been wiped clean. The person forgiven no longer has to bear the burden of guilt. The person forgiving no longer bears the burden of resentment.

There is also the pertinent question here of self-understanding and self-forgiveness. An insight about this has been very helpful to me. Just as I must make an effort to be gentle and forgiving in my dealing with others, so must I extend this same gentleness and forgiveness to myself. I am so complex that I cannot accurately judge myself or be sure about the extent of my responsibility. I'm not suggesting that we cop out with some projection like: "The devil made me do it." I have to be willing to accept responsibility for my actions and the effects of those actions. Still it is difficult to be certain about my subjective intentions. I am a fraction and the roots of my motivation are all tangled.

However, I can face the fact that my actions have been disordered and may have inflicted some harm on others. How responsible I was subjectively for those actions will always remain something of a mystery, even to me. Therefore, even though I must accept my responsibility, at the same time I must continue the effort to understand and forgive myself. In any case, an apology to those whom I have hurt, by commission or omission, remains very much in order.

When I first began teaching, it was in a high school for boys. Of course, we beginners were saddled with the advice from the veterans. "Don't smile till Christmas." "Don't be nice. They will take advantage of you." "Always stay in control." On the first day of class I was mildly terrified. And in retrospect I think I spent the whole first year of teaching wondering about how well I was doing. I tried to teach well, to be fair, to be strong. But it was all designed to establish my success as a teacher. In fact, I think I can honestly say that I used those boys to make me a success. I did not look into their faces to ask, "How are you doing?" My total preoccupation during that first year was, "How am I doing?"

Years later these young men had an anniversary reunion, which I was invited to attend. When asked to say a few words, I gratefully accepted: "I really need only two words to say what has been on my mind and in my heart for a long time now. *I'm sorry.*" At this point there was a ripple of laughter. However, I insisted, "Hey, I mean it. And if you don't take me seriously this time, I'll have to come back to your next reunion and make the same speech." I told them of my regret that I did not think more about them and their needs during those early years. I admitted that I was scared and self-centered. I concluded my apology with: "I am sorry that I was not more of a person when I first met you."

At the same time, I acknowledge that I am a being in process, that "God is not finished with me yet." I am not about to dissolve in a sea of regret that I was not perfect when I began my teaching career. I have to be gentle with myself, to withhold all harsh judgments. At the same time, I needed to say what I did to those young men. There was a feeling of "release" after I said it and they accepted it. I felt that the record had been set straight. Later one of "my boys" wrote me a note. He told me about the warm and good feelings he had in my class. He reassured me that he felt he was speaking for all the others. Somehow the matter seemed closed. I think we were all released from our burdens by my awkward apology.

Sometimes we have to stretch to say "I'm sorry," but the almost miraculous effect it will have on communication and on our relationships will make the effort seem more than worthwhile.

And a happy *ho'oponopono* to you and yours.

22

We must avoid a buildup of tension.

Quiz:

1. Do little things irritate you?
2. Do you have trouble sleeping?
3. Do you wake up in the morning feeling tired and grouchy?
4. Do you worry a lot?
5. Do you feel trapped?
6. Are you a frequent complainer?
7. Do you often snap at those who are closest to you?
8. Do you suffer frequent physical symptoms (headaches, indigestion, rashes, and so on)?

Note: If you answered "yes" even to one of the above questions, you may well be experiencing a buildup of tension. (Having established that, please proceed.)

The members of Alcoholics Anonymous are warned by the word *HALT* that danger of relapse into destructive drinking might be imminent. *HALT* is an acronym for Hungry-Angry-Lonely-Tired. Hunger, anger, loneliness, and fatigue can easily throw us off balance. They can have a definite effect on our emotional and behavioral reactions. In a similar way, a buildup of tension in us is also a flashing red light. It can be a warning signal that danger is imminent. We are in danger of saying or doing something that could easily prove destructive. It may well tear down our lines of communication and even destroy our most precious relationships. The general word for all the pressures that can throw us off balance is *stress.*

Have you ever watched a tightrope walker? Maybe you noticed the use of a "balance bar." Ever so carefully the performer moved the bar from side to side in order to maintain balance. Now, life is something like this for us. You and I are negotiating the difficult, if different, courses of our lives. Life means action, and action means other people. Other people mean that there will be some friction, and this friction often results in stress. Some of this stress is helpful and positive. Some of it is negative and harmful. We badly need our balance bars.

Most of us have learned to recognize periods of stress only by uncomfortable physical symptoms or behavior that is difficult to explain. Such unusual symptoms can often be explained by a buildup of tensions or harmful stress. Clinically, what we call "stress" is a reaction of the human body to stimulation. When tension or stress builds up in us and continues over a long period of time, we get the uncomfortable feeling that we are "under pressure." We become irritable. We quickly get into counterproductive arguments. Things that ordinarily don't bother us begin to feel like "the last straw." We flare up when things don't go right. We grit our teeth when the train pulls out just as we are arriving at the station. We curse the driver who cuts us off in busy traffic. We easily blame others for our own mistakes.

The internal wear and tear of prolonged tension is humanly destructive. Our emotions become overactive. Our nerves feel frayed. Our immune system turns off under tension, and we get sick. The late Dr. Hans Selye, the world-recognized authority on stress, maintained as a certainty that stress plays some role in the development of every disease.

Here and now we are interested, however, in the effect of this negative stress upon communication. The pertinent fact is that excessive tension *distorts reality for us.* Sometimes when a person has had too much alcohol, we comment, "I think it's the wine speaking, not the person." In a similar manner, when a person experiences a buildup of tension, and reality is bent out of shape, we can in the same way conclude, "It's the tension speaking, not the person."

Most of us tend to ignore the buildup of tension resulting from the negative stressors in our lives. We usually advert to tension only when a so-called "target organ" (the head, the stomach, the skin, the back) sends us a distress signal. We develop a headache, a stomach upset, a rash, or pains in the lower back. The body is doing its best to warn us that pressures are building up. Or we might lose our appetite or begin to eat ravenously, depending on how we react to tension. Almost always we tend to "overreact" because reality has been distorted and we have lost our perspective. The slightest noise becomes unbearable. The most innocent teasing is interpreted as persecution. The molehills of life begin to look like mountains. We tend to say things we don't mean, to misinterpret the intentions of others. We see everything through a magnifying glass. And while we are in this state, it is difficult for anyone else to talk us out of our interpretations and reactions. We become unreasonable, but we're sure that we are right.

There are quite a few suggestions on the market for managing stress successfully. Eat a balanced diet, avoid too much alcohol and nicotine, make space in each day to practice a "relaxation response" or transcendental meditation, take time out to indulge in a hobby, rid your life of rush and clutter. Some have suggested that the management of tension should be holistic, should affect all our parts. Therefore, it should be approached:

Physically—by getting physical exercise and eating a balanced diet.

Emotionally—by expressing all our significant feelings at the time we are having them.

Socially—by phoning a friend, having a party, getting together with people we like.

Intellectually—by feeding the mind with reading, doing a crossword puzzle, attending a lecture.

Spiritually—by admiring the beauty of the world, listening to music; by spending ten minutes a day meditating or praying.

All seem important, but I would like to discuss here only the first two recommendations. I think that they are the most neglected. They are (1) *physical exercise* and (2) *emotional openness.* First let's talk about the effects of *physical exercise.* The traditional formula for tension is "an overactive mind and an underactive body." When we burn off the buildup of tension with a daily walk, some brisk jogging, a sweaty game of racquetball, or an energetic swim, we clean out of our brains and bloodstreams the biochemicals of tension. At the same time we clear out the channels of communication. We become much more capable of quiet reflection. We return to being "ourselves." We enjoy a restored sense of balance. We stop snapping and start sleeping. We begin to accept the various situations of life more tolerantly and peacefully.

Other common recommendations for physical exercise are: climb stairs instead of riding an elevator or escalator; park a half mile from work and walk the rest of the way; take lunch hour walks; jump rope for five minutes; do stretching exercises or calisthenics. One very successful executive admits that he relieves himself of pre-board-meeting tension by five minutes of calisthenics in his private office.

In recommending exercise, the experts always caution us to proceed with guidance from a physician. It is good and necessary advice. But I want to urge you to do whatever you can safely do. Don't listen to the sedentary scoffers or the lawn-chair directors. Move your muscles. And be sure to notice how the exercise restores your mental and emotional perspective. More than ten years ago I took up jogging. It has made an enormous difference in my life. One day before my morning run I talked with someone on the phone. After the run it seemed quite clear to me that I had been edgy and a bit difficult in the pre-run conversation. So I called the same person back and asked if this was true. It was confirmed for me: I had been exactly what I suspected. But after the hour's workout, I was a different person. I felt more "in charge" of my reactions and of my life.

The second preventative I would like to underline is *emotional openness.* Much of our stress comes from pent-up or bottled-up emotions. Sometimes I think of the process of suppressing our feelings as pushing down on an emotional spring. To do this we have to hold the spring down, which requires a prolonged effort. It is not at all hard to imagine that such a strenuous process results in tension. When the tension finally becomes unbearable, our emotions suddenly explode. The spring won't be held down any longer. Spectators at such an emotional explosion are usually baffled. They are totally unaware of the previous prolonged effort at suppression. They didn't notice the increasing strain to hold the spring down. They only wondered about the sudden and unexpected eruption.

Most people are agreed that the body is a biological computer recording everything that goes on in us. When we cram our feelings down into the basement of our guts, we may fool others, but we don't fool our bodies. Our nervous systems and our muscles know all about our foolish efforts. The nervous system becomes agitated and the muscles grow strained and taut. We take out on our poor tense bodies what we refuse to speak out in open communication.

The practice of this emotional openness which we are here proposing will eventually result in two very valuable abilities: We will learn to *identify* our negative stressors and we will be able to *reevaluate* them. As mentioned earlier, stress of itself can be either a positive or a negative force. It's like the tension in a violin or guitar string. If it is too tight, it will snap. If there is no tension, there is no music either. And so, stress in itself is neutral. However, our reactions to it, based on our personal beliefs and values, are what give a stressor either a positive or a negative power over us. The biological computer of the body often helps us differentiate. However, if I examine my daily life by listening to and learning from an open expression of my emotional reactions, I will slowly locate and learn to identify the negative stressors in my life.

For example, I will notice strong tensions when I am in a success-failure situation. Or I will perceive that any form of conflict with another person gives me a headache. Also, it has been suggested that we get angry only when our expectations are not met. I may well discover that I am placing unrealistic expectations on myself and on others. Or I may notice that deadlines always upset me. A recent article in a psychological journal suggests that our perspective on "time" rules our lives. Some of us live in the past, some in the present, and others only in the future.

We take out on our poor tense bodies what we refuse to speak out in open communication.

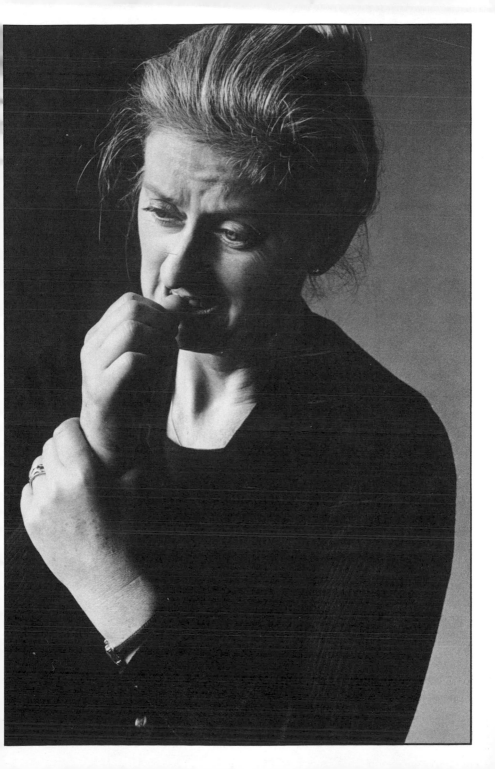

Or I may discover, through listening to my emotional reactions, that I am forever insisting on personal perfection, or perhaps I am trying to please everyone all the time. In other words, under every emotion lies an attitude: toward success, conflict, expectations, time, perfection, pleasing others, and so forth. However, I can uncover and explore these attitudes only if I am willing to experience and to express my feelings. I've got to welcome, acknowledge, and express these feelings before I can learn from them.

Then comes the revision or reevaluation that can convert a negative stressor into one that is positive. I can reevaluate the obnoxious qualities in another as "cries of pain." I can recognize that true success is doing my best, whatever the results. I can reevaluate conflict, and see it as a chance to learn. I can come to the realization that I don't have to please others. What I have to do is be my true self. A parent can learn to see in the nonconformism or even rebellion of a child an effort to become independent. This reevaluation process has been called the art of seeing a promise in every problem. As the old Roman philosopher Epictetus used to say, "It isn't your problems that are driving you crazy. It's the way you look at them."

So have your feelings, own them and express them. And above all, learn from them. As Matthew Arnold once said, "Resolve to be yourself, and know that he who finds himself loses his misery."

The avoidance of a buildup of tension will surely make communication a lot easier. It makes life a lot easier, too!

23

At times of crises in communication we will need to use special approaches.

At this point you might be asking yourself, "What about those times when nothing seems to work?" And there truly are times when all efforts to communicate do seem futile. All of us experience breakdowns in communication now and then. It's part of relating. To say it will never happen would be to deny the facts of life.

Those breakdowns do not necessarily signal the end of a relationship. They are simply communication crises. They are much like situational crises when a person is temporarily overwhelmed by an event. In the relational crises of communication one or both persons are overwhelmed. I may be overwhelmed either by the other person or by my own internal reactions. For example, another person's anger may appear so frightening to me that I am unable to communicate. I don't want to put my head in the mouth of a roaring lion. Or in the process of communication I may be overwhelmed by my own feelings of inadequacy.

When we are overwhelmed—either by situations, other people, or by something in ourselves—we are unable to function effectively. At such times we are unable to communicate effectively. Our usual methods of speaking and listening just don't seem to work. We feel frustrated, helpless, and sometimes hopeless. We say things like, "We're back to zero again . . . It's no use . . . Nothing works." Or perhaps, "I don't know what to do. We're going backward, not forward in our relationship." Or we might say to ourselves, "It will never get any better. We're passing like ships in the night. And I'm just tired of trying. I give up." Do any of these statements sound familiar?

First and foremost, my *attitude* toward such crises will have a considerable effect on the *outcome* of the crises. If I think there could not and should not be communication crises, I will often be painfully surprised as well as frustrated. This, of course, is true with all unrealistic expectations. If I construct imaginary and romantic versions of reality, I will always be disappointed by the real thing. And then my disappointment and frustration will breed a sense of futility. The crises that do occur will seem like the end of the line to me.

I will be spared much of this gloom if only I learn to accept crises as a normal, inevitable part of communication. After all, two absolutely unique persons are trying to share their very different and highly personalized views of reality. The fact that communication often works is almost more amazing than these occasional crises.

Second, it is very important not to view these inevitable crises as failures. Otherwise we're digging another hole of disappointment for ourselves. If I consider a crisis to be due to a failure on your part, I will blame you. However, if I attribute the failure to myself, I will probably focus on my own wounded spirit and become guilt-ridden and defensive. It is much healthier to view a communication crisis as an opportunity to stretch, change, and grow. If I take this view of crises, all kinds of positive emotional energy will be available for me. My energy will not be wasted on blaming or self-recrimination. Then I can honestly say to you and to myself, "So this is what they mean by the ups and downs of life. Well, I'm gonna hang in there with you, and we're gonna make it together."

In order to work through these crises profitably, it's important to understand when and why they occur. Sometimes they are simply a natural part of the growth process.

The emotional lives of all human beings move through cycles of intimacy and distancing. It is normal and natural. The entire world of nature evolves through cycles in the growth process. If I accept this cyclic evolution, I will be able to work within it in creative ways. I will recognize crises as milestones of growth. I will see these crises as chances to be creative rather than as catastrophes of destruction.

Not all crises, however, are part of the growth process. Some crises occur because of the way I (or you or both of us) communicate. I may not have mastered one or another of the essential skills of communication, which are called "guidelines" in this book. There are many ways to fall from good communication into a crisis. One of the more common ways is to stop using "I statements" and to begin making "You statements." If I fall into this trap, I will soon be directing, labeling, judging, or blaming you. We will no longer be on level ground moving toward each other. I will distance myself from you.

Another surefire way to create an instant crisis is to throw up an emotional smoke screen by pouting instead of coming right out with, "I feel hurt." Also, what are called "hidden agendas" are inevitable flames under the kettle of a crisis. I tell you, for example, I want only to share my thoughts with you. However, my hidden agenda reads, "Get even with him. On the scorecard of win-lose contests, you are losing." Or I may claim to want only a chance to express my feelings. Instead, however, I rip you apart with my rage. Obviously, hidden agendas make for a crisis time.

It is a crisis of another color when my emotions become too intense for me to experience and express. To protect myself from what I interpret as "too hot to handle" emotions I will put on a mask that conceals my real feelings. Of course, real communication will abruptly stop here. For example, something you are sharing with me makes me wonder if you might be thinking of rejecting me. If I am extremely sensitive to rejection, I will act quickly to prevent it. Instead of telling you about my fears, I may whip out and put on the mask of Penny Pleaser or Danielle the Distractor. The real me will have to go into hiding. Finally, some crises occur when one or both of the communication partners are not really listening to each other. Advising, assuming, judging, or any of the standard blocks to listening always results in a communication crisis.

Before suggesting ways to meet a communication crisis successfully, let me first encourage early recognition of a crisis. The sooner we become aware of a crisis in communication, the easier it will be to handle. Remember, we're not interested in assigning blame to either one of us. We simply want to identify the crisis. Then we can try to work our way through it together. If communication begins to feel forced and tense, we should ask ourselves these questions about the process:

1. Are we using "You statements"?
2. Are emotions being acted out indirectly rather than expressed openly?
3. Are we ventilating or manipulating rather than communicating?

The entire world of nature
evolves through cycles in the growth process.
If I accept this cyclic evolution,
I will be able to work within it in creative ways.
I will recognize crises as milestones of growth.

4. Does either of us feel emotionally overwhelmed?

5. Do we sound defensive? Are we being defensive?

6. Are we keeping score on an unseen scorecard?

7. Are we into a blame-counterblame pattern?

8. Are we falling into the traps of advising, assuming, or judging each other?

9. Does mutual and open listening seem blocked?

10. Do we feel frustrated by our exchanges?

If we answer "yes" to any of these questions, we need to do three things: (1) go into slow motion, (2) shift the focus from the issue to the process, and (3) analyze the process together.

For example, one might say:

I'm feeling bewildered by this exchange. Could we slow down a bit? I'd like to sort out with you what's going on here between us.

Notice the "I statements," the self-disclosure of a feeling and the absence of blaming. Also the speaker is expressing a sense of responsibility to do something about the crisis. All these features are very important to include. Otherwise the suggestion of the focus shift from the issue to the process might be misinterpreted.

What questions are pertinent to the analysis? Certainly we should ask: Are we both talking about the same issue, or have we been going separate ways into different topics? Are we both really committed to communication on this issue? Do we have the right motivation for good communication? Is this the right time for both of us to discuss the issue? Do we agree about the nature and the process of communication? Are we both being honest and open with ourselves and with each other? Despite the fact that there are several questions here, this can all be done very quickly. The effort is mainly designed to locate the stress point. Then we have to agree on needed adjustments. After this, we can resume good communication.

Analyzing the process can usually untangle a communication crisis in its early stages. It can also help turn a full-blown crisis into a growth experience. The analysis will help us recognize our patterns of communicating as well as the detours we tend to get into. We can definitely learn and grow from this knowledge.

However, we may not foresee a crisis. Or once it is upon us, we might not be able to make a breakthrough. Still there is no need to panic if we are flexible and creative. If the slow-motion analysis doesn't work, there are other approaches that can be very helpful. For one thing, we can admit and agree that we aren't communicating very well. Then we simply need to accept ourselves as being somewhere between here and there on the journey of growth. In other words, we are "in process." We can also arrange a "time-out" with a to-be-continued clause. Often time and distance help us achieve a new perspective. There is no law that says that all communication must be completed in a single sitting.

Another crisis-breaking device that many people find effective is letter writing. The Marriage Encounter movement has promoted and taught this method of writing "love letters" as a guarantee of ongoing communication. Even if letter writing is not routinely used, a crisis point may be an excellent time to try it. As always, with good communication, letters should contain only "I statements." Personal details of observations, thoughts, and feelings should all be included in such letters. These letters might well focus on the issue itself or on the stalemate of the communication process. Letters used to clear the air should deal with behaviors and reactions, without an argumentative or judgmental tone. Also, it is wise to limit the content of these letters to the here and now. They should not be a resurrection of past issues. Finally, the tone should always express respect and gratitude and, wherever possible, true affection. Here is a sample composed by us:

Dear Andrew,

I'm still upset that our conversation last night ended so negatively. I guess I felt uptight when I thought you were changing the subject of our conversation. In fact, I felt some anger rising up in me. I didn't express it at the time because anger frightens me. When it is my own anger, I don't know how to express it without just dumping it on you. Anyway, I froze and I pulled away from you. I wish I had told you all this last night. I'm truly sorry that I didn't. Maybe we could have sorted things out on the spot. I would really like to try again, and talk this out whenever you feel ready. Thanks for being there, even if we are at a distance emotionally.

With much love, Maria

No guideline would be complete without a few well-placed warnings. We should spend some time together regularly with our partners in communication. However, we shouldn't overdo it. In other words, we should spend enough time together in sharing, but marathon sessions are exhausting. Excessive and intensely sustained conversation can make us tense and driven. And overly serious worrier-types are usually poor at sharing. We need balance in our lives: enough work, enough play, enough rest, and of course enough real communication. We have to be involved with all the facets of a full life.

Also, we have to be careful not to close out an issue either too soon or too late. If we close out too soon, it is usually because we are uncomfortable with the subject or with the emotions we experience while discussing it. When we do this, we create "forbidden issues." We put up "Do Not Trespass" signs. We let fear control our dialogue and our relationship. All this will limit our relationship and our personal growth.

On the other hand, some of us don't know when to stop with an issue. We continue to exhaust the subject and ourselves. This will almost always discourage communication by making it an unpleasant experience. If there is more to be said, remember that there is always another day.

Many of us take our communication for granted. We talk and listen, and so we assume that we are really communicating. We don't really work for improved communication. Then a crisis in communication occurs with the suddenness of lightning and seemingly out of nowhere. It catches us off guard and we have no resources to meet and survive such a crisis. It is important for all of us to regard the communication process to be just as essential to full living as eating and exercise. In relationships it is communication that sustains life just as surely as physical food and rest sustain physical life. We try to eat nourishing food and get sufficient rest in order to be healthy and fit. We also need to give serious attention to communication and its required skills so that our relationships can be healthy and thriving.

Perhaps the best preparation for an unexpected crisis is to have in place an established, ongoing communication process. This should be a built-in part of every relationship. Where this is a fact, all kinds of skills, procedures, and attitudes are available sources of help. Naturally, we believe that the best way to do this would be to reread and practice all twenty-five guidelines suggested here. If we keep this up, we will eventually "own" them. If and when they become an integral part of our communication, we will then be well equipped to meet and to work through any crisis.

The Chinese word for *crisis* has two characters. The first means "danger," and the second means "opportunity." Here's hoping that all your crises will not prove dangerous to the health of your relationships, but will instead become opportunities for growth.

24

Whether speaking or listening, the motive of the good communicator must always be love.

A good working definition of interpersonal love is that of psychiatrist Harry Stack Sullivan: "When the satisfaction, happiness, and security of another is as real to you as your own, you truly love that person." This desire to see you satisfied, happy, and secure is *not* just a feeling. Feelings are instant, transient, and ambivalent. Love is rather a *decision* (I am going to love you) and a *commitment* (I will say, do, and be whatever you need for your satisfaction, happiness, and security). In other words, I decide that I am going to love you as I love myself. And I am going to provide as best I can whatever promotes your true happiness.

This is what love is. And this is the love that must be the motive of all communication. Like many other things, a motive can be recognized by its consequences or results. "By their fruits you shall know them." If my motive is love, the first thing I will do is to observe you, to look at you with the supersighted eyes of love. Love is not really blind; it is supersighted. A loving person sees things in another that nonloving eyes can never see. I make this observation of you in order to read your moods and recognize your needs. On one day you may need me to celebrate a recent success with you. On other days you may need me to sit silently with you in a dark room of grief. It may be that you will need my tenderness at times. At other times you may need my toughness. But whether you need blue velvet or blue steel, I will try to supply it.

In trying to love you, I may even offer you a gift of love which you may not want or appreciate. I may think that love asks me to challenge you or confront you. This may not be easy for either of us. However, if my motive is really love, I will try to say and do and be whatever will promote your satisfaction, happiness, and security. But please be patient. There will be times when I am uncertain, when I will hold out my gift in trembling hands. I ask you to believe that I am offering this gift because I love you and want whatever is best for you. And also, please be forgiving. There will no doubt be times when my own pains will overpower my best intentions, when I will act selfishly, when I will do and say hurtful things.

But true love, if it is rightly understood and if it is my motive force, will always offer these two gifts:

1. The gift of myself in honest self-disclosure.
2. The gift of yourself by contributing to your awareness of your own unique goodness and giftedness. This is my contribution to your self-esteem.

At times it may seem that these two gifts are incompatible. If I am angry at you or feel hurt by something you have done, I owe you this honest self-disclosure. If I try to keep it bottled up inside myself, I will act it out in stupid, immature ways. I will always be harboring a hidden agenda. On the other hand, if I tell you of my anger or my hurt, even if I own them and take personal responsibility for them, such disclosure may not promote your self-esteem.

There is no easy answer to this dilemma. It will certainly help if I do own and accept responsibility for my reactions, whether appropriate or inappropriate. It will likewise help if I make it clear that no judgment of you or your intentions is implied. However, I think that the rest of the dilemma must be resolved by trust in human intuition. If I tell you of my anger or hurt—*not* in order to make you feel bad or to get even with you, *but only* because I want you to know me—I think you will realize that. You will intuitively recognize my sincere and loving intention.

Those occasions when confrontation seems in order also present a difficult situation. There could well be times when I see you on a self-destructive course and feel the need to confront you. Obviously before doing so I should honestly evaluate my motives. If I am confronting you and challenging you to change so that it will be easier for me to deal with you: that is not love. That is manipulation. If I am confronting you and challenging you to change because I think that you will be much happier: that is love. But once I have checked out my motives, I will have to rely on your intuition to know that my confrontation is intended as a gift of love.

In any case, it is no doubt much better for me to tell you of my anger or hurt and to confront or openly challenge you. I know that I would rather have you be open with me. I would

Love is not really blind; it is supersighted.
A loving person sees things in another
that nonloving eyes can never see.

rather have your anger, hurt, or challenge out in the open where we can deal with it. The only alternative is to leave me guessing, and to leave you bottling up your thoughts and feelings. Again, what we don't speak out we act out. So if you don't level with me, your suppressed thoughts and feelings will probably take the form of pouting, distancing, or wall building. Whatever is not openly expressed in a relationship becomes a subtle force of destruction.

Sometimes it is difficult to know what is the loving thing to do, to say, to be. Each of us is a profound mystery. It is not easy to read another's mood and recognize another's needs. At times I will be flying blind. Sometimes love is blue velvet—tender and gentle. Sometimes love is blue steel—firm and tough. Consequently, love is an "art," not a science." There are no hard and fast scientific formulas guaranteed to produce definite results. Love is a delicate art that requires many sensitive decisions. Sometimes love leaves us filled with doubts, somewhere between a rock and a hard place. We wonder what love would have us do, be, or say.

At times I have thought that it is much easier to know what love excludes rather than what love requires. However, once more a loving intention is recognized by its deeds. The motive of love would clearly exclude:

1. Hurting or punishing you.
2. Retaliating for something you have done.
3. Putting you down, back into your place.
4. Getting you off my back by closing you out.
5. Keeping you at a distance.
6. Manipulating you to feel or act in a way that would please me.
7. Ventilating, dumping my "emotional garbage" on you.

8. Refusing to listen to you.

9. Building walls between us.

10. Ridiculing, chastizing, judging, or competing in order to surpass you.

In his First Letter to the Corinthians, Paul tells us what love is and what love isn't, what love does and what love does not do. Of the ten things listed above, Paul would say, "Love is not like this. Love doesn't do these things." "Love," he says, "is patient and kind, never jealous or envious, never boastful or proud. Love is not haughty or selfish or rude. Love does not insist on doing things its own way. It is not irritable or touchy. It does not hold grudges. Love is loyal: it hangs in there with the one who is loved. It looks for what is best, and stands firm in defending the person who is loved" (paraphrasing is ours).

Finally, there is one other common misunderstanding about the meaning of love. Most of us fear that the decision-commitment of love is like volunteering for "doormat duty." Sometimes it seems that it should be very easy for others to take advantage of a loving person. The truth is that love is not a synonym for naiveté. One of God's central commandments is to "love our neighbor *as we love ourselves.*" A proper love of self always enters into good communication. And love of self would never tolerate being used or abused. Love of self does ask me to go out of myself to read your moods and recognize your needs, but it doesn't ask me to let you become a domineering tyrant or an emotional bully. That would not promote either your happiness or my own.

If someone were to begin to abuse me verbally, or try to manipulate me, to treat me as a doormat or a dingbat, it would neither be loving myself nor loving that person to smile sweetly and turn the proverbial "other cheek" for more punishment. It is true, I am sure, that the only formula for human happiness is to become a loving person and to make one's life an act of love. This is the supreme and universal beatitude. But this does not mean that we are invited to crawl through a long and dark tunnel on bleeding hands and knees. "The glory of God is a person who is fully alive," according to Saint Irenaeus. To become an underdog in a human relationship, to invite or accept inhuman treatment, to become a thing of convenience for another is neither the fullness of life nor the way of love.

The contents of this book have been divided into twenty-five guidelines or directives for good communication. In a very real sense they are also twenty-five guidelines or directives for loving oneself and others. To quote God's word once more:

> *Make love the rule of your life*
> *and you will be very happy.*
> John 13:17

And a happy life to you and all those whose lives you will lovingly touch!

25

We should pray for the enlightenment and the courage to communicate well.

God has always been big on what is called "petitionary prayer." Augustine once called petitionary prayer "our greatest strength and God's greatest weakness." The Lord assures us: "Ask and you will receive; knock and it will be opened to you. Whatever you ask in my name will be granted to you."

In fact, I have often thought about God as being like an electrical outlet. Behind every outlet is the mysterious power of electricity. It can light a room, heat a home, show a movie, and so forth. However, the outlet is literally useless unless we get plugged in, connected to the source of power. The power of God, we are assured, is ready to enlighten our darkness, mend our brokenness, fill our emptiness, brace our courage, straighten our twistedness, and create in us hearts of love. The connection of all this power is prayer. The psalmist assures us: "The Lord is near to all who call upon him" (Psalm 145:18).

We need God's help in many ways, but certainly we need God's special help if we are to live lives of love. Paul instructs us to pray for all of God's gifts, but especially to ask for the gift of love (1 Corinthians 12:31). It has been wisely said that love works for those who work at it. Love is not dropped from the heavens as a prefabricated, wrapped-in-cellophane gift. Love is a do-it-yourself kit that requires daily effort. And the central effort of love is communication. In a real sense love is communication. Both ask us to share generously with others the unique goodness and giftedness that is ours. Both ask us to receive gratefully the shared goodness of others. For this we clearly need God's help.

To summarize briefly the demands of communication, please read over just the titles of the various guidelines proposed in these pages. Communication requires of us:

1. A firm commitment to sharing.
2. An attitude that sees ourselves and others as gifts to be given and received.
3. A relentless honesty with ourselves.
4. Acceptance of personal responsibility for our actions, reactions, and lives.
5. A humility that knows that we can tell only *our personal* truth, that we cannot claim to have *the* truth.
6. Emotional openness: an honest sharing of all our significant feelings.
7. A willingness to share our own vulnerability.
8. A heart that is grateful to others for their willingness to listen.
9. A gift of presence and availability to others.
10. Acceptance of others, wherever they are.
11. Listening to learn the inner consistency of others.
12. The knowledge that we cannot judge others.
13. A gift of empathic reactions to others who are different from ourselves.
14. The effort to understand not just the words but the meaning of others; to listen with head and with heart.
15. Our gift of independence to others by refusing to give advice or to make decisions for them.
16. The clear-sighted courage that overcomes all the blocks to good communication.
17. An explicit expression of thanks to those who have trusted us enough to share with us.

18. Faithfulness in spending "quality" or "special" time together.

19. Communicating through the sense of touch.

20. Stretching out of our comfort zones.

21. Admitting our failures and apologizing to those we have hurt.

22. Avoiding a buildup of physical tension and negative stress.

23. Dealing effectively and courageously with our communication crises.

24. Speaking and listening always and only out of love.

25. Consistently asking God to supply us with the enlightenment and courage we need.

You may stop holding your breath now. Quite a challenge, isn't it? Most of us will have to unlearn old, destructive habits and acquire new life-giving habits of sharing. We will have to change, and change is always a little scary because we know what we've got and we can't be sure about what we will get.

Alcoholics Anonymous has been by far the most effective means of recovering sobriety for millions of men and women who have become addicted to alcohol and other drugs. The heart of the program is summarized in "The Twelve Steps." It is ironic that only the First Step mentions alcohol. The other eleven, directly or indirectly, refer to a "Power greater than ourselves" or "the God of our understanding." It is presumptuous, I suppose, but I would like to suggest the Twelve Steps as a paradigm, or model, for those of us who want to be honest and open in our communication. (Please be patient with me, okay? Thanks.)

The Twelve Steps of Alcoholics Anonymous

1. We admitted we were powerless over alcohol—that our lives had become unmanageable.

2. Came to believe that a Power greater than ourselves could restore us to sanity.

3. Made a decision to turn our will and our lives over to the care of God as we understood him.

4. Made a searching and fearless moral inventory of ourselves.

5. Admitted to God, to ourselves, and to another human being the exact nature of our wrongs.

6. Were entirely ready to have God remove all these defects of character.

7. Humbly asked God to remove our shortcomings.

The Twelve Steps of Noncommunicators Anonymous

1. We admitted that we were powerless and estranged from others in our lives. Our relationships had become unmanageable.

2. Came to believe that a Power greater than ourselves could restore to us true communication and relationships.

3. Made a decision to turn our will and our ability to communicate over to the care of God as we understood him.

4. Made a searching and honest inventory of our relationships and commitment to communication.

5. Admitted to God, to ourselves, and to one other human being the masks we have worn, the roles we have played, the lies we have lived.

6. Were entirely ready to have God remove our masks and roles, to restore us to honesty and openness in our communication.

7. Humbly asked God to remove our obstacles to communication.

8. Made a list of all persons we had harmed, and became willing to make amends to them all.

8. Made a list of all persons whom we had hurt by withholding an honest sharing and a loving listening, and became willing to make amends to them all.

9. Made direct amends to such people wherever possible, except when to do so would injure them or others.

9. Made direct amends to such people wherever possible by an honest apology and a request for forgiveness.

10. Continued to take personal inventory and when we were wrong, promptly admitted it.

10. Continued to observe ourselves in the communication process, and when we failed in some way, we promptly admitted it.

11. Sought through prayer and meditation to improve our conscious contact with God as we understood him, praying only for knowledge of his will for us and the power to carry that out.

11. Sought through prayer and meditation to improve our conscious contact with God as we understood him, praying only for the enlightenment and courage to communicate openly and honestly, to know and to be known.

12. Having had a spiritual awakening as the result of these steps, we tried to carry this message to others and to practice these principles in all our affairs.

12. Having had a spiritual awakening as a result of these steps, we tried to share with others the meaning and value of honest and open communication and to practice it in all our relationships.

Finally, I would like to conclude our own sharing in this book with a type of prayer that has helped me very much. I would like you to try it. It requires that you go into a quiet place and practice whatever you know about the techniques of relaxation. Deep breathing, imagining holes in the bottom of your feet with a soft, cool breeze blowing up through them, repeatedly and rhythmically saying the word *relax* as a command to your mind and to your body. Please do whatever helps you the most.

After five or more minutes of relaxing, move into what is called "positive imagining." On the screen of your imagination run a homemade movie of yourself as you would like to be. Because I tend to be a "Type A," driven and intense, I imagine a peaceful person who seems to know what is important and what isn't. Since my act is to be a helper and therefore to "have it all together," I like to imagine my ideal self as someone who is utterly honest and who can laugh at himself. As you know there is an ancient Chinese proverb which reminds us: "Blessed is he who can laugh at himself. He shall never cease to be entertained."

Of course, my ideal self is an incarnation of the guidelines presented in this book. He is utterly honest and open about himself. He tells it like it is. He assumes responsibility for all his emotions and behavior. He listens sensitively and empathically. He is generous in sharing his gift and he is grateful for the shared gift of others. He is demonstrative and he dares to step beyond his comfort zones. He is, in sharing and listening, an excellent communicator.

I have done this so often I have him memorized and would know him anywhere. Sometimes I feel like the little boy in Nathaniel Hawthorne's story "The Great Stone Face." You will remember that this boy throughout the days of his

"Is this the person I would like to be?"

childhood admires a face he sees etched in stone high up on the side of a mountain. When he grows up, he finds that the face is his. He has become his ideal. At the end of my own "positive imagining," an exercise that should be repeated regularly, I ask God to empower me to become all that I can be as a communicator. I ask the God of my understanding to let my ideal transform my reality. I want to be a generous sharer of God's gifts and a grateful receiver of the gifts and goodness of others. "Create in me, O God, a loving and listening heart."

Then in various moments of my life, when I am relating to and communicating with others, I observe myself in action, and I ask, "Is this the person I would like to be?" I sincerely hope that this will help you as much as it has helped me. For me it is almost like taking a truth serum or putting on a new pair of glasses with the right prescription for clear vision. I find the simple question, "Is this the person I would like to be?" a transforming question. It is impossible for me to ask that question and stay huddled in my comfort zone, to be petty or pouting, to show off or try to pass myself off as someone I know that I am not.

With this question I quietly ask God to help me become my ideal. I ask God to empower me to practice what I preach. Help me to be real. If I am not real, I am nothing. My life will only be a charade. I dread this thought, that death will come to me like the final curtain of a command performance. I will then wipe off my stage makeup, take off my costume, give back my lines to the author, while the audience continues to applaud me for being someone I never was. I know that when I come to die, God will look for scars, not medals. When I am dying, I want to remember the times when I was real and honest, when I shared myself in an open self-disclosure as an act of love. I want to remember the times when I gave to those who were hungry the food of my sharing, to those who were thirsty the drink of my listening and understanding, to those who were locked inside themselves the gentle, extended hands that said, "Come out. You will be safe with me." I want to remember the times when I offered the healing gift of loving and caring to those who were sick.

It sure beats a charade.

Thanks for letting us share
these thoughts with you.
May your life be happy and full.
And please remember us
as loving you!